iHuman
User Guide

iHuman
User Guide

written and illustrated by
Paul Hawkins

ALBATROSS

For anyone who ever shared a car, a couch or some kindness

Copyright © 2016 by Paul Hawkins
All rights reserved.
Albatross Publishing
First Edition
ISBN 978-0-9569656-2-2

Released in German as 'Gebrauchsanleitung Mensch: Bedienung, Wartung, Reparatur', Verlag C.H. Beck, 2014
(ISBN 978 3 406 66891 3)

Also by the Author:
Dealing with Adulthood: A Handbook for Newcomers, Late-Starters, and the Poorly Integrated (Upcoming)
How to Take over the Earth (Upcoming)
Visit www.paul-hawkins.com for more about the author.
Visit www.hencewise.com for big ideas and little jokes.
Facebook: facebook.com/hencewise/
Twitter: @hencewise
Email: paul@hencewise.com

Hello and welcome,

You're operating a *Human*.

Firstly, thank you for choosing the very latest model of shaved and upright monkey-style primate as your preferred method of experiencing the planet Earth. We know that there were simpler models of life-form available (snail, tree, germ, etc.), and we appreciate that you have opted to spend your time in one of the more 'with it' branches of the family tree. We also hope you'll agree that recent developments in *Brain, Thumbs & Bipedal Erection*™ technology make your Human one of the most fun animals it is possible to be as you experience everything that there is.

Indeed, unlike Earth's other vaguely sentient creatures - which must spend their entire lives *eating* and *trying not to be eaten* - the modern Human experience is famously light of nature's old and boring problems, which should allow you to focus on making your life as nice, complicated and ridiculous as possible instead. Indeed, through a unique combination of advanced features - such as thinking, guessing, hands, and remembering - your Human has the potential to do an almost unlimited amount of things that other animals just can't.

For example, while operating your Human, you'll get to...

... *create stuff!*
With your unique imagination, you'll be able to invent things only a Human could possibly care about, such as Fridays, toasters, swearing, London, and the moustache.

... *experience pleasure!*
Being essentially outside of the food chain means that your Human will get to experience many enjoyable, non-essential kinds of activity, such as 'fun,' 'spare time,' 'brunch,' 'giggling,' 'lay-ins,' and more.

... transfer knowledge!
Have a weird, abstract idea in the privacy of your own head? Shout it out loud! Watch as it bounces from your brain into someone else's, and becomes real life confusion.

... be modern!
As a Human that exists *now*, you get to exist on the rather convenient receiving end of history's privilege. No need to figure out *fridges*, *soap* and *wifi*, you can just start using them like a futuristic genius!

... make jokes!
A human, a cow and a duck walk into a bar. The barman asks, "what is this, some kind of joke?" The animals just make noises, of course, but the Human alone says, "um, it certainly seems like it... the only thing it's missing is a punchline." This is because humans alone understand what jokes are.

... ponder!
Hydrogen? Magnets? Reality? Cushions? What's all that about? Operating a Human is like being a curious, emotional computer on legs, and there's a whole baffling and freaky universe to bumble around in.

All this... and much, much more!

These trickier functions are, of course, what makes operating a Human so uniquely complicated. This is why you can't just point one blindly in the direction of society, slap it on the bum, and hope for the best.

Instead, your Human will require regular maintenance, careful optimisation, skilled operation, and at least the occasional morning reassurance that its hair looks fine. If properly cared for, however, no other species offers as much incredible potential for entertainment, cheekiness, fun, novelty value, and even fulfilment. This manual will show you how.

Please enjoy your Human as much as you possibly can. Thank you.

Contents

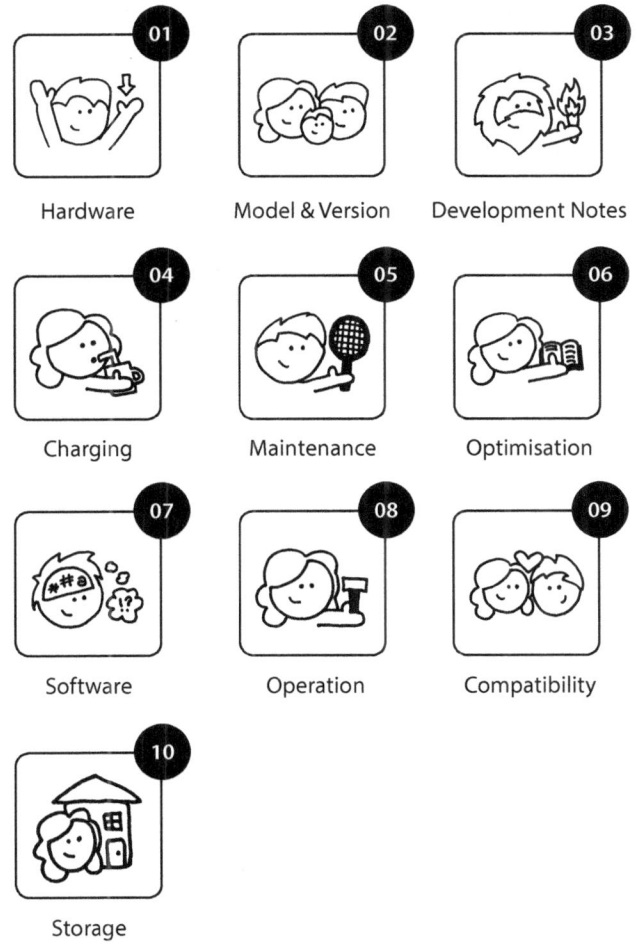

01. Hardware
02. Model & Version
03. Development Notes
04. Charging
05. Maintenance
06. Optimisation
07. Software
08. Operation
09. Compatibility
10. Storage

Hardware
Using Meat-Based Technology

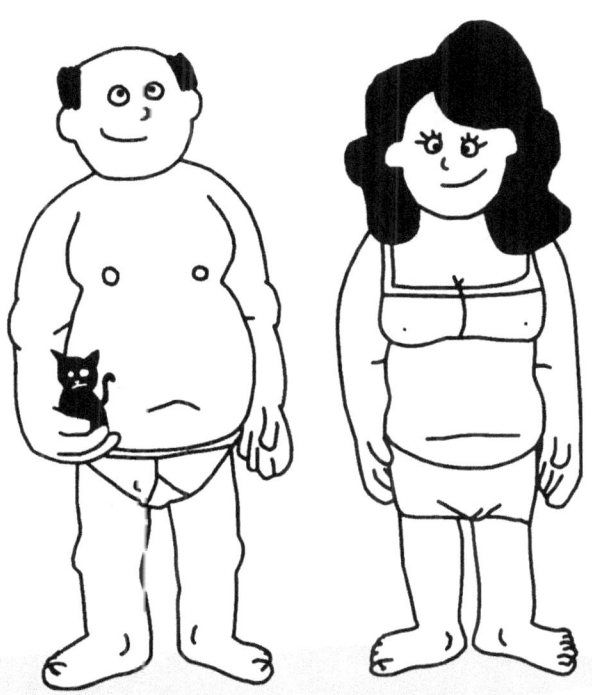

Features: At a Glance

From the vantage point behind your eyes, you should be able to get a good overview of your Human's primary features. Looking down, you should notice feet and hands tapering upwards into arms and legs, arms and legs tapering upwards into a torso, and a torso tapering upwards into the nothing where your head should be. This is normal. If seeing your body *below* your legs makes you concerned that your Human is upside-down, you can investigate the issue by removing a shoe. If it doesn't hit you in the chin, you are still the right way up and sensibly alligned with gravity. Bravo. A closer inspection should also reveal the following:

Feet are ugly, less useful leg hands. They have three main characteristics. They are long and flat, allowing you to balance your Human in an erect and action-ready position. They are far away from the nose and eyes, freeing them to be smelly and ridiculous. Finally, they are shoe-shaped, so they can be easily hidden in shoes. This prevents the smell and a bit of the ridiculousness for most of the day.

Arms are the main part of your Human, and are essential in the majority of high-end tasks. Ending in hands, they are the primary body part used for eating, washing, pointing, flailing, and handling tools. Because arms are the busiest part of the Human, they are also the part most likely to get caught in a big wheel.

Hands are in between fingers and arms, and act mostly as a plate for the storage and transfer of objects, like cats. In previous models of Human, fingers only had to perform cruder functions that required less dexterity, such as thumping, mashing, scooping, and shovelling. More recently, however, they have been upgraded to more effectively deal with a reality that is 90% using buttons.

Thumbs are one of your Human's most special features, because they operate the keyboard's space key, and are 'opposable,' unlike the thumbs cows don't have. No Human has ever used the term 'opposable,' incidentally, except in the context of their thumbs, which is at least half of the reason that they are so special.

Legs are for transportation only, and are only really important because they get the arms where they need to be. This is why some models of Human are increasingly replacing perfectly reasonable legs with engines, wheels, and chair-based weight gain.

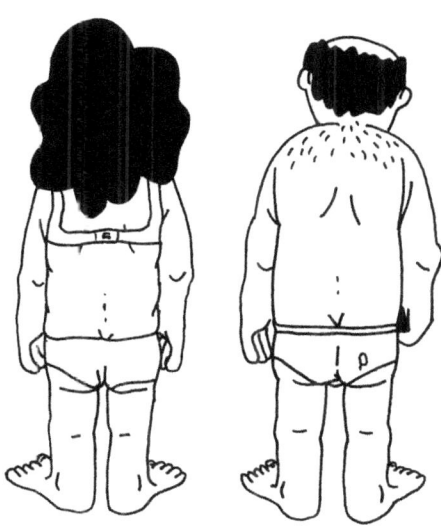

PICTURED: YOUR HUMAN'S LEAST IMPORTANT SIDE

Genitals are the most important part of the Human, because they are where the majority of the most important and maybe even life-changing decisions are made. Genitals, of course, come in two distinct types: there are the ones which vaguely collaborate with the brain, and ones that don't. Which type you have determines your gender.

Knees help you change your Human's position. When not in transportation, knees have two settings: *180 degrees*, ('laying'), where they are recharged for the next day's erectness; and *90 degrees*, ('sitting'), where they generally wait for something. Humans spend 95% of their time in these two positions, and the other 5% getting from one to the other in a some form of high-velocity chair launcher (car, train, plane, etc.)

Shoulders are needed for carrying bags, pressing phones against ears, and for being things that arms attach to. They are also instrumental in shrugging, which your Human can use to *not care*, except theatrically.

Armpits are the busiest hinges on your Human's body, which means they must sweat for lubrication. Being closer to the face than the feet and the bum, it is the responsibility of the armpits to inform the nose when a Routine Clean-Up is neccessary.

Bums are two in-built cushions for sitting. While constantly divided, they work well together, probably because they get to sit with each other so much. The middle of the bum contains a mouth, which is primarily used to release waste, but can also say a single smelly word that Humans pronounce 'fart.' It is probably their favourite word, especially when the bum says it loudly.

Accessories

PROTECTIVE CASE

To live in different habitats, you must dress your Human in various kinds and shapes of cloth, mostly according to the temperature nearest to you. Humans who live in hot places normally tend to wear less, which attracts tourists.

DOCKING STATION

Sofas and chairs are places for you to rest your Human in the daytime. Unlike beds, sofas are for when you want to quickly restore a little energy, but keep your brain just turned on enough for television, conversation, and noticing intruders.

CONNECTIVITY DEVICE

Most models of Human now carry a mobile telephonic device (this is what the cool kids are calling them) because it has two important functions: Firstly, it allows you to connect your Human with other Humans, no matter how far away they are; Secondly, it allows your Human to ignore other Humans, no matter how close they are, by giving you something you can pull out of your pocket and jab with your thumbs until the other person is gone.

ACCESSORIES

You can use your wallet or purse to store the most important little souvenirs from your Human's life and government. As well as carrying cards to prove one's own identity, it is not uncommon to also carry old photos of loved ones, to remember wistfully what they no longer look like.

Keys have two magical abilities. Firstly, the ability to open houses; secondly, the ability to disappear once inside those houses. There are lots of different kinds of key, which allow you to regularly go back to the same house without worrying that you will find unexpected Humans living in it.

ACCESSORY BAG

You might also consider carrying a bag, which is an easy way to transport more stuff than you could possibly fit into just your hands, whilst allowing you to bypass the inconvenience of having to kick that stuff along the ground in front of you. Bags can be used to carry almost everything, except a lot of things, such as caravans, porcupines, and soup.

ADD-ONS

Your hands are optimised for the handling of tools, which means it is very easy to change the purpose of your Human at short notice, simply by putting something new in its grip.

PICTURED: THIS HUMAN HAS BEEN GIVEN A SPANNER, AND IS NOW OVER-QUALIFIED TO BREAK A BICYCLE.

The Face: At a Glance

Your Human's head not only holds the brain and the tongue, but is also covered in many points of interest, which are often combined into a single concept called *your face*. Every Human's face is arranged slightly differently, which is how those Humans generally remain unable to recognise over seven billion variants of each other.

KEY FEATURES

Eyes are for looking, seeing, watching, noticing, and staring. They are also important in judging and finding. They must be kept wet at all times by a process called *blinking*, preferably in a synchronised way (doing just one at a time is called *winking*, and is considered old-fashioned, cheeky, creepy, or sleepy.) Eyes are sensitive to light, sadness, and poking.

The nose is for pre-testing whether things are edible or not. The nose has two modes: *smelling* and *breathing*. Unlike ears, eyes, and eyebrows, your nose doesn't have a matching partner, so it often feel completely alone on the face. There is also the lonesome mouth, of course, but unfortunately noses can't hear mouths, because noses don't have ears.

Mouths connect Humans' brains to each others by making noises. They are also for *eating* and *breathing*, two essential processes that allow you to continue talking without losing weight or suffocating. Sometimes, mouths live underneath the brush-like novelty of a moustache, which can improve the experience of food by adding the dimension of tickling.

Tongues are powerful muscles which are used for getting food out of teeth and licking. They are mostly wet, and can therefore be combined with substantial bravery to put out fires.

Teeth are another high-tech accessory, engineered so you no longer have to gum, mash, and flob your way through three portions of solid organic matter a day. Teeth are not good for wine, coffee, and cigarettes, which is why Humans who drink and smoke a lot prefer to have bad ones.

Hair never stops growing. Unfortunately, though, it is one of the main visual indicators of social groups, which means that you must regularly cut your Human's hair into the same shape, so that you can always be recognised by your correct tribe of friends and relatives. It is falls out, it is replaced by a haircut called *baldness*.

Ears are the opposite of mouths. Some people say because Humans have two ears and one mouth, they should listen twice as much as they speak. These people should be reminded that Humans also have one mouth and two legs, meaning they should probably shut up, and go away.

FACE DESIGN NOTES

How your Human's facial features are organised and displayed will, perhaps unfortunately, determine most of your position on the underlying hierachy of attractiveness which society functions on:

VERY UGLY	Oh dear. Better develop some talents.
BELOW AVERAGE	Ideal for radio.
AVERAGE	Ideal for use in a police line-up.
ABOVE AVERAGE	Ideal for bar work.
VERY BEAUTIFUL	Personality optional.

WARNING: BONES

It's just about true to say that bones are not *exactly* designed to be broken. However, they *do* heal *and* grow back stronger, which means - for the courageous and lazy opportunist - they present a very immediate, sustainable, exciting and ever-present opportunity to get out of doing things you don't want to do.

Most Humans prefer to break their bones when *skiing*, as holidays are a great way to leave work, and *hospitals* are a great way to avoid coming back. If a skiing holiday is out of your price range, however, then falling should be considered as a great, low-budget alternative.

Joints turn bones into hinges. Joints look vaguely similar but have very specific jobs, so they can rarely be used interchangeably. The elbow joint, for example, is well-configured to bring food to the mouth, whereas the knee joint isn't close enough, making it hard to get food much further than the thighs. Indeed, if food is going "straight to your hips," you should consider changing the way that you eat. Try using your arms instead of your legs, you maverick.

Components

Inside your Human is a complex technical set-up: a silent, organic engine made up of many different gooey organs digesting things, pumping things, and converting useful things into useless things, and back again.

Because you can not see your Human's organs, however, it is normal to spend less time worrying about them than your hair, body shape, and armpit odour. Unfortunately, it is only possible to notice problems with your organs when it is too late to prevent them, so it is best to treat them reasonably if you can, just in case you need them one day for a picnic.

Organ	Purpose	Maintenance Required
HEART	The heart is a beating pump that keeps the inside of your Human lubricated by flushing it with blood and wetness and oxygen and love.	A healthy heart should be able to beat to various tempos. To exercise, it can be sped up with the administration of coffee, running or terror.
SKIN	The skin protects your Human from bacteria and over-heating, and is also the main barrier preventing them from reverting to a more inconvenient and soup-like existence.	It is helpful to look after your Human's skin and treat it kindly, as it has the ability to produce spots and pimples in quite a vengeful way on special occasions when you're likely to be photographed for posterity.
LUNGS	The lungs are self-automated body balloons that suck in air from outside, and keep it inside your Human. This is to prevent your Human from being squashed by gravity into a person-nonsense-pancake.	Lungs need oxygen, which is why it is common for many Humans to keep plants as pets, despite them being the most boring pets imaginable. When lungs stop working, Humans become so heavy that they must lie down forever and melt.

STOMACH	The stomach is for digesting food, rumbling, and speedily reversing poor decisions involving tequila.	Stomachs are easy to monitor as they have various warning sounds to indicate problems. Generally the louder, wobblier and more ridiculous the sounds, the more advised you are to proceed to a bathroom far away from polite company.
BRAIN	The brain is for digesting information from the eyes, ears, nose and mouth, and turning that raw data into ideas, plans, stereotypes, distractions, creativity, and confusion.	The brain requires plenty of nutrients and mental exercise to ensure it does not become forgetful, soft, gullible, irrational, forgetful, repetitive, boring, boring, or boring.
KIDNEYS	Humans are manufactured with two kidneys, but only need one to clean blood and make wee. This makes the kidneys a very popular organ to give away.	If you've selfishly kept both of your kidneys, most doctors strongly recommend trying to get shot in the kidney. Indeed, the only thing they recommend more is not getting shot at all.
LIVER	The liver is the Human's enjoyment regulator, possessing the ability to convert wine and sausages into corresponding levels of hangovers and obesity.	Livers are incredibly durable organs. A healthy diet and limited alcohol intake are therefore the easiest ways to waste your liver's true potential.
GUT	The intestines are the biggest and longest of all the organs. If you could take the intestines out of the body, and stretch them from end to end, your Human would not survive.	The intestines are an important part of ensuring waste food gets from the stomach back to outside. Blockages should therefore by regularly checked by swallowing some butter and coins.

Common Malfunctions

Unfortunately, your Human's hardware remains susceptible to occasional but inevitable glitches and malfunctions. These are called *illnesses*, and they are generally caused by tiny, invisible, airborne things called *germs*, which are transferred by bigger, more visible, less airborne things like children.

Germs are completely unavoidable, but your Human will gradually build up a stronger immunity to them. Once a Human body has been sick from one kind of germ, indeed, it can never be sick from that kind of germ again. In purely mathematical terms, this means that the more germs that attack you earlier, the less that can attack you later.

Consequently, very sickly adults are often just the by-product of children who weren't allowed to eat mud and get sick at all. This is why naturally disgusting children should be left well alone in their unhygienic pursuits. Any child sucking on an old frog they've just found under a bin is obviously on a clear trajectory to becoming one of life's winners.

Children whose parents use anti-bacterial cleaning products, meanwhile, are more likely to grow into the kind of weirdos that over-use sprays which claim "to kill 99.99% of bacteria," but nonetheless live in constant fear that the last 0.01% has a personal vendetta against them. Incidentally, these people are rarely so genocidal towards the 100,000,000,000,000 bacteria living rent-free inside their intestines.

One of the main illnesses that could affect your Human is 'the common cold', which mostly causes a malfunction of the face: noises, puffy eyes, nose explosions, and a confused emotional state that suggests, "Yes, I'm too poorly for interaction, using a computer, and work, but no, I'm not quite poorly enough to waste this opportunity for attention, computer games and guilt-free laziness. *Cough.*"

The common cold can not presently be cured, and so is best treated with a period of rest. This is especially important for the most male versions of Human, who run the unique risk of their colds developing into full-blown man-flu, which causes the kind of devastating sniffles that only the most heroic and valiant of very masculine personalites can overcome.

Before you rest, your first priority should be to inform everyone around you that your Human has officially become *unwell*. Now, fellow Humans at school or work can avoid you. Alternatively, if they want to avoid school or work, they can find you, lick you, and also become sick enough to stay at home and play video-games.

Trouble-Shooting

> PROBLEM: MY HUMAN WON'T GET UP IN THE MORNING.

Is your Human fully charged?

You should first try turning your Human off and on again - by turning your alarm clock off and on again - to check that your Human's hardware is fully charged. If your Human will not respond to stimuli - such as water, drum kits, and manhandling - it may not yet have enough replenished energy to *get up*. On the contrary, if it opens its eyes and leaps straight into a canal, it is well-rested and possibly even over-eager for the day.

Has your Human accepted reality?

Sometimes, you will struggle to *get up* because your Human was having a nice dream, and you subconsciously believe that there is a good chance of going back to that dream, even though there definitely isn't. Weirder still, even if your dream was incredibly boring - and just involved you counting jars as they swam past your submarine up a chimney - your Human will always have a strong urge to revisit the nonsense scenario and finish the job.

Is your Human's hardware functioning properly?

If your Human is fully charged and has accepted the sensory evidence that *reality* exists again, you should check if there are any obvious problems with its hardware. If you can't feel your legs, for example, it is possible that you have woken up without arms. Meanwhile, if you're not sure whether you can feel your arms or your legs, you might have woken up without a head. This is quite a serious condition, as it can seriously dampen your ability to understand what the problem is.

Is your Human's functioning hardware refusing to function?

Sometimes, your Human's hardware will simply refuse to function due to unhelpful levels of comfort. If you could theoretically move all of your limbs, but you are using most of that energy to curl yourself into a duvet-covered hedgehog-shape while swearing at the universe, your Human is not yet ready to accept that morning has arrived again.

No? Don't worry, your Human just has a healthy, overwhelming hatred of mornings.

Many models of Human simply hate mornings, believing them to be confusing and unnecessary prefixes to The Day. Waking up to a ceiling and a universe that is completely beyond their comprehension, it is not uncommon for your Human to become immediately distracted by questions like, 'is that a spider in the corner?', or, 'what is existence?'

This situation can be improved by giving your Human's life a 'purpose'. Tried and tested 'purposes' include jobs, pets, tin-opening, being right, and children.

Models & Versions
Upgrades and Downgrades Available

Genders

In order to avoid not-existing forever, Humans must reproduce. This is done through the mediums of sex and babies and the passing of DNA from one generation to the next like it's a precious midnight kebab.

Your Human is therefore most likely to come in one of two different, complimentary shapes. These are called *women* and *men*.

After you have figured out which kind your Human probably is, you are then encouraged to reproduce by finding a 'partner' of the opposite 'gender.' Women are generally, but not definitely, encouraged to find men. Men are generally, but not definitely, encouraged to find women. This system is statistically simple, mathematically simple, and infinitely complicated.

Indeed, despite there being exactly equal amounts of both genders everywhere, Humans can destroy all of the inherent simplicity of nature's 'mating process' by substituting it for the invented complexity of a 'dating proccess.' Essentially, this man-made system involves *not* sleeping with the nearest available opposite, but instead trying to sleep with *the best* nearest available opposite that they think they can.

This procrastination, of course, is mostly due to vanity.

Essentially, most models of Human are oddly, instinctively delighted with their own DNA, which means they have a strong natural instinct to try and pass that exact DNA on to their children. However, current models of Human are not yet able to simply clone their own DNA and begin immediately popping out an army of exact, miniaturised replicas of themselves, however much they would like to. This manufacturing quirk is partly to encourage genetic variety, but mainly to reduce the risk of people who refer to themselves as 'Wacky Henry' existing more than once.

Instead, Humans must reproduce in a much more complicated way, by mixing half of their DNA with half of the DNA of someone else, through a giggly or sincere process of suddenly bumping into each other a lot.

Because they can't just clone themselves as they would like to, Humans instead try to find the best possible partner that they can, in order to at least minimise the risk of diluting their own good looks and winning personality. Thus Humans pair up with each other depending on how much they love themselves.

In terms of personality, men and women would be almost identical, if they could be kept apart from each other for long enough. However, they do have minor differences in their hardware, which are listed below:

Feature	Notable Differences
BRAIN	Male and female genitals are different, complimentary shapes, but they also behave slightly differently when stimulated. While the female vagina remains gracious, in-keeping with the general dignity and significance of its role, the penis tends to act a bit more like a Labrador who keeps hearing the word 'SAUSAGES!' come from two conflicting directions at the same time.
EMOTIONS	Existing models of Human have a very confused view about how emotional sensitivity is distributed between the sexes. While it is almost entirely balanced, the popular perception is that men have a spectrum of just two emotions - hunger and revenge - whilst women are creatures mostly controlled by the position of the moon.
	In fact, both genders have the same native potential for emotion, it's just that men are culturally more likely to blame those emotions on the existence of a nearby onion or obscure them in a rambling metaphor about the organisation of a tool shed.

SIZE AND STRENGTH	Men are ever so slightly bigger than women, which has historically been enough to convince themselves that they should be in charge of everything.
	The positive side of this, if there is one, is that men have sometimes accidentally achieved things as a by-product of them constantly competing like dim puppies for women's attention. On a local level, this is done by subconsciously comparing penis size through the mediums of sports, cars, beer, and lifting. On a larger scale, however, this same instinct drives progress in society, as men try to impress women with their bigger air-planes (penises), cars (penises), bank accounts (penises), space rockets (penises), stadiums (testicles), and penises (penises).
	The downside is that men haven't always driven society in the right direction. Indeed, mostly they've just gone in any direction, as fast as they could, without any help, and only asked for directions at the point that they'd totally forgotten where they were trying to go.
REPRODUCTIVE ROLES	Women are the most important kind of Human, as they are the only kind that can manufacture more Humans inside them. Meanwhile, men feel so completely useless during pregnancy that they are famous for having bad ideas like war and golf.
	This imbalance of power between men and women is only beginning to be addressed in modern times, mostly because Humans have managed to freeze semen, negating men's final teaspoonful of usefulness. Now men have slowly started to apologise to women in the hope that they might be allowed to stick around in a future rightfully belonging to peace-loving lesbians.

Development

Your Human will develop over time in distinctive stages. These stages are mostly defined by height and usefulness, but are often classified in society by something called *age*.

Your Human's age will be determined by scientists based on how many times you've made another full 940 million kilometre lap of the sun. Most models of Human agree that every time the earth is in the same cosmic position as it was when you were born, you are one 'year' older and deserve some cake. This is called your *birthday* (although, more accurately, it is the anniversary of your relationship with Earth.) Some models of Human even collectively agree on how many laps of the sun you must make before your status can be upgraded from *child* to *adult*, no matter how tall or useful you are.

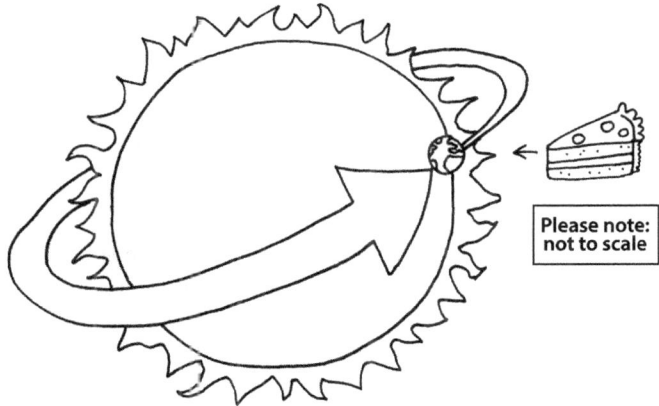

Please note: not to scale

Adults have important roles in Human society, such as the abilities to pay taxes, pay taxies, drive taxies, and vote. Despite this, no system exists as yet to demote adults back to the status of children, even if they do not seem like they are responsible enough to care for a pot plant without somehow exploding a nearby shed.

BABIES

Babies are the initial larvae stage of the Human. They are small, silly, and regularly unprofessional. Their primary concerns are *noises* and *leaking*, which they try to do from all holes, at all times, pausing only occasionally to fall unbelievably asleep.

Unlike other animals on Earth - which have to deal with significant predators because they are not born in a natural habitat of blankets, grandmothers and cuddles - babies can and do remain almost entirely useless for as long as possible. For about two years, indeed, a baby Human's highest priority is trying to figure out the greatest amount of foot it can fit into its own mouth.

Because they are too young to be sent up chimneys, their only real economic value is a type of cuteness that can be used in adverts to sell bottled water. This is even true of the ugliest babies, although you have to be a bit more thirsty.

Babies are essentially genderless, but evolve into either boys or girls.

TODDLERS

Toddlers are babies that have learnt to crawl with increasingly less arms, and been rewarded with wider access to things they can put in their mouths.

They are mostly identifiable by their impractical height, the plompy yet confident nature of their walking, and their incredible greediness. Indeed, it is not uncommon to see a toddler trying to pick up a hedgehog, eat a mobile phone, fall into a river, and bonk a girl on the head with a big rubber hammer, all at the same time, while riding a tricycle.

Despite the diversity and grandness of these over-lapping intentions, however, often the only assured outcome is that they will achieve none of them, to a spectacular degree, yet still somehow manage to bang their head on a corner.

CHILDREN

Children are more highly developed models of Human, possessing both the ability to run and ask questions - two complimentary skills which allow them to not understand anything, but faster. This learning process officially begins at the symbolic point that a toddler uses the hole in the middle of the toilet for the first time. While it might sound trivial, it is the precise moment when your Human is both physically developed enough to *aim*, and mentally mature enough to *choose to*.

From this day on, childhood is generally spent running around at great, clumsy speeds, falling out of trees with increasing regularity, pointing inappropriately at anything that moves, and shouting 'WHY?' at the nearest adult any time something happens.

Children come in two main types, which are more visible from the toys they are given than their appearance or mannerisms: *boys* (short hair, naughty), mostly get given toys with wheels or guns, and *girls* (long hair, naughty), mostly get given toys that cry and wet themselves.

The two opposite models of child do not always play well together, sometimes believing the other type to be *yucky*.

TEENAGERS

This is roughly the age when children realise that adults know absolutely nothing, and grow spots on their face in protest. Having spent an entire childhood figuring out the basics of how the world around them works (numbers, seasons, magnets, etc.), teenagers finally feel comfortable enough to start thinking about what's going on inside them.

They soon discover that this topic - *themselves* - is endlessly fascinating. It being the first time that they've noticed who they are, however, this can cause some initial minor confusion. Unfortunately for them, this often coincides with the rather inconvenient moment that *who they are* begins suddenly, irreversibly mutating, twisting any initial minor confusion into a greasy, turbulent, decade-long melodrama of awkward shape change, embarrassing voice squeakiness, and antisocial hair growth.

The opposite gender of teenager, meanwhile, is seen increasing less as *yucky*, but suddenly, bizarrely, weirdly, confusingly, importantly, frighteningly *unyucky*. They don't initially know why they want their attention or how to get it, but the pursuit to figure it out will often involve hair gel, cinemas, alcho-pops, trauma, the internet, and rumours.

ADULTS

Adults are the tallest model of Human, and are therefore expected to do everything that isn't fun.

This could be a daunting new challenge for the inexperienced, unemployed Human, but luckily lots of institutions already exist to help new adults start not having fun, including workplaces, tax offices, and banks.

To keep adults content with the horrible deal the world mostly offers them, they are given a reward called 'money' every time they do something that isn't fun. This 'money' can then be swapped for everything that is fun and isn't money, like books, cheese, chairs, holidays, and bricks, which are often arranged in a way that keeps all of the other stuff they've bought safe from the wind.

In between doing everything that isn't fun for stuff and money, an adult's second task is to find another unyucky adult to share all their stuff and money with. Trying to find and keep a good one soon takes up most of their remaining time, leaving only a little bit to figure out how they are eventually going to answer children's questions. This is roughly the point they realise they can't.

Luckily, children don't realise this, so generally adults keep telling them that magic fairies are going to come when they're asleep to buy their old teeth, so go to bed now, please.

ELDERLY PEOPLE

Growing old is not a privilege granted to everyone, so the elderly should be cherished for the walking, whimsical windows they provide into the world as it was before you arrived in it. They also have two main roles in society.

The first is *wisdom*, which is like advice, but older. This can include both timeless pieces of sound-thinking, like "a penny saved is a penny earned," but also more dated and confusing suggestions, like "in my day, a loaf of bread was a real loaf of bread. It cost four shillingsworth of pennyfarthings and three cockneybits of tripe. You don't know you're born."

The second is *pottering*, which is a relaxed and conclusionless style of walking. Pottering, at its most mild-faced and unhurried, should suggest either, 'I have done everything. I have seen everything. I am content,' or, 'My knees are swollen. My teeth are missing. I am lost.'

Elderly people have the most free time of any kind of Human on Earth because, unlike adults, they already own everything it is possible to own, so they no longer need to do anything to earn the money to buy it. Furthermore, unlike children and adults, they are no longer forced to go anywhere to waste their entire daytimes.

The downside of the latter is that they often don't get the chance to understand cutting-edge developments in thinking, and sometimes fall behind with technology. The upside, of course, is that they get to remain in a wonderful bubble of euphoric ignorance, perfectly assured that this new world of blinky, bleepy computer-phones is much worse than the one they grew up in, where they still had to ride a borrowed bicycle to the village sundial just to make sure they weren't late for a war.

Development Notes & History

Naturally selected for ultimate comfort

Development History

The model of Human you are operating is a *Homo Sapien Sapien*, which is considered by many critics to be the most full-featured version of the upright-shaved-monkey-thinking-primate-type-mammal available. It's double *Sapien*, so you know it's good.

The most notable difference between the current model of Hominoid and its predecessors is the upgraded brain capacity. In particular, there has been significant expansion of the pre-frontal cortex feature, just behind the eyebrows, which gives this model of Human the unique abilities to plan, have a good memory, predict consequences, solve problems, notice patterns, and have a good memory. It is mostly this uniquely snazzy brain that gives your Human all of its massive amounts of potential.

While there may seem like an almost infinite number of ways to optimise the operation of your Human, however, there are also certain biological limits that are hard-wired in, and which must be taken into account. These are best summarised as *laziness* and *greediness*.

To avoid expecting too much from your Human, it is worth remembering that these two characteristics are essentially pre-programmed survival techniques, both cultural and biological in origin. The natural world has always rewarded these two attributes greater than any others, which is why they have survived, thrived, and flourished. The opposites of laziness and greediness are, of course, *doing stuff* and *giving things away*, which never helped any one survive. In the meantime, *laying around on the couch all day eating endless handfuls of cake* never killed any one (quickly.) Sometimes evolution is that simple. People who stay in bed the longest have the greatest odds of multiplying, after all.

In order to understand your Human's natural instinct to do as little as possible, whilst nevertheless demanding the greatest reward for it, you must understand that it developed to do two main things:

1. Figure out which tasty-looking bunny rabbit was closest.

2. Figure out how to make someone else go and fetch it for you, whilst you laid around instead and scratched yourself.

Fast-forward hundreds of thousands of years, and you'll find that these two entirely understandable compulsions have now become pretty deeply etched into the default Human personality. These two traits are slightly more problematic in modern life, however, since the world is no longer a place where mostly nothing happens and then once a month you see a rabbit. While this aspect of ancient life had previously given greediness and laziness a vaguely self-regulating aspect, in modern times it is now possible to sit only in a beanbag, and get almost infinite amounts of terrific food delivered directly into your mouth, just as long as you can figure out which internet-connected device is closest, and how to make someone else go and fetch it for you.

List of Previous Upgrades

Listed below are the major turning points in the development of your Human's body, brain, existence, and confident attitude towards nature:

LIFE

There's a controversial *bang* of some description. Later, single-celled organisms decide to exist, then become dinosaurs, then not dinosaurs, then are cheeky monkeys with thumbs. This takes a while.

MONKEYISM

Monkeys used to live in trees, mostly because dinosaurs didn't. It was safe, and there was fruit. Once dinosaurs stopped existing, the idea of occasionally leaving the forest became more appealing. *Walking around* replaced *getting eaten*. Meanwhile, it was no longer necessary to have so many hands and fingers, so nature kindly converted some of those hands into longer, flatter hands to balance on, and some of those fingers into toes, for wiggling, stubbing, and counting beyond ten.

CAVEMANISM

Some monkeys invent fire, then decide to re-brand as Humans. As *cooking* develops, *salad* and *dying young* become increasingly unpopular.

NOMADISM

Upon realising that fire converts slow, boring cows into quick, delicious steaks, Humans begin migrating all over the earth to follow animals and put them in their mouths.

PROPERTY AND OWNERSHIP

Soon tired of running around after animals in order to eat them, Humans invent *fences*. Fences keep animals in. Soon, fences keep Humans out. This ends the problem of lunch getting away, and begins a different problem of who the lunch "belongs" to.

MONEY

The problem of who "owns" what gets worse as people decide that two apples are worth one orange. Money is invented to help them swap one apple for half an orange. Money is very, very clever, but causes at least ten thousand years of problems (ongoing.)

Meanwhile, particularly rich and powerful people build huge monuments to themselves - like statues, palaces, and pyramids - perhaps in the hopes of cultivating future tourism. To do this, they mostly use other people's money, which they cunningly negotiate from them with weapons. However, in a remarkable twist of generosity, they let the other people look at the monument from far away several millennia afterwards, as long as they're behind a bit of red rope.

SETTLING

With fences in place, Humans decide it's easier to just sit down in one location and cover themselves in bricks. They build houses near rivers, and mostly find that this style of life is less stressful than moving their entire camp every time a gazelle hears a noise. Humans decide to settle, and build wells, markets, sewers, bins, bin-men, and multiplex cinemas.

TOWNS AND CITIES

Settlements expand to the point where they must be given names, and every one in the countryside is politely asked to live in them so they can spend the rest of their life in a factory, please. Nature, meanwhile, gets so far away that people forget it's there unless they see it on a postcard.

ELECTRICITY

Humans invent *electricity*, which is fire you can switch on and off. It takes a while for electricity to be widely adopted as the new medium of heat and light exchange. This is because the Candlelight Industries believe that modern Light-bulb technology undermines Candlelight Producers and Distributors' profits, and decide to sue any one who illegally downloads light directly into their home.

Notes On Evolution

In order to understand why your Human is not always as smart, pretty, or functional as you would like it to be, you must understand that people did not come fully-formed and perfect from magic forest space eggs.

No. They were an accident. They *evolved*. They are just another one of nature's clumsy, ongoing experiments. Humans come from monkeys, and monkeys come from smaller monkeys, and smaller monkeys come from cats, and cats come from dogs, and dogs come from insects, and insects come from germs, and germs come from what scientists call "the confusing bit." When this happens in roughly the correct order, this is called *evolution*.

Evolution works on a principal called *natural selection*, which means nature helps select for you attributes that generally make you less likely to stumble into a ditch and die. Generally, if you are born slightly more useful than your parents, you are slightly more likely to survive, and then slightly more likely to have slightly more useful children, maybe.

This apparent 'progress', when first studied, can seem counter-intuitive, as if evolution had chosen to be on humanity's side. When sand went in their eyes, they got eye-lashes. When they needed to hold stuff, they got thumbs. When they wanted to bend, they got knees. This has led some models of Human to the pleasant but effortlessly wrong conclusion that things are getting better, and better, and better.

Unfortunately, this is a misconception. Evolution didn't gradually chisel your Human into the most optimised, magical shape possible... it just threw a lot of messy stuff at a wall, and quite a lot of it stuck.

Adaptations don't need to be perfect, good, or even better; they just have to be stubborn. Like eyebrows. Indeed, an evolved thing is merely the sum of the maximum possible number of mistakes that could be made while still allowing not all of that previous thing to die.

For now, Humans roughly function, which means there is little incentive for nature to change them more. In addition, some models of Human believe that the existence of contraception, dating sites and increasingly charitable standards have put a stop to the process of natural selection, by helping to nullify some of the processes that would normally filter out the gene pool. Like most pools that don't get filtered, there is a good chance that the remaining genetic contents of humanity will gradually become pretty gross.

However, this theory does not take into account humanity's ability to change their environment from something they're adapted to, to something they're not adapted to.

This is why, in pursuit of an exciting challenge, most Humans are busy trying to melt the Earth.

Design Notes

Some of your Human's attributes evolved for environments or situations that you are no longer likely to be involved in. Because it would take too long for these redundant modules to evolve away again, however, their specifications have mostly been re-imagined as follows:

Component	Old Purpose	New Purpose
EYELASHES	Keeping sand and predators out of eyes.	Fluttering; catching snowflakes in a romantic and irritating fashion
EYEBROWS	Keeping sweat and predators out of eyes.	Expressing emotions like scepticism, surprise, intrigue, and bewilderment.
WISDOM TEETH	Chewing leaves, roots, nuts, and meats.	Upsetting your jaw, smile, face, and mood.
FEET	Hands.	Feet.
FINGERS	Poking things into mouth-hole; holding sticks; dropping sticks.	Typing.
MALE NIPPLES	?	?
APPENDIX	Digesting grass.	Randomly exploding.

WARNING: RACE

As Humans are friendly, curious nomadic creatures, you should not be afraid to meet ones that appear slightly different to yours, as not all models of Human look exactly the same.

This is because the Human family was temporarily separated on different land-masses for a brief few hundred thousand years, and their bodies responded in slightly different ways to suit their slightly varied habitats. Some got lighter skin and some stayed dark, mostly depending on where they lived, and how much the sun was trying to burn them.

Despite these minor differences being normal, boring, sensible, and generally as trivial as a widowed ant's anniversary plans, some Humans were slightly surprised to meet up with each other again and find out that they had become different colours. Indeed, there was even a few minor historical blips when one "type" tried to own another "type." Luckily it was soon agreed that this wasn't a nice way to treat a people that were also a people.

In more modern times, all kinds and colours of Human try to coexist together in peaceful harmony, united in their hatred of wasps.

Charging
Restoring Power on-the-go

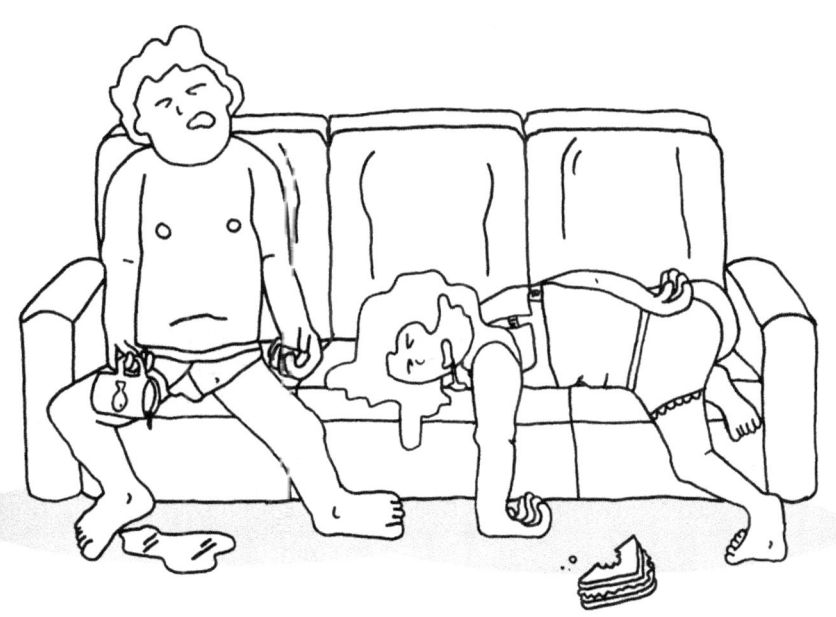

Sleeping

After a long day of being a Human, your Human should be turned off and recharged. Energy must be restored to the body and the brain through a resting phase called *sleep*, which involves not dancing and not concentrating.

(The only exception is when Humans sleep *with each other*, when they concentrate a lot on a strange kind of horizontal wrestling dance that exerts a lot of energy. The purpose of this wrestling is mostly to gain strategic control of the duvet. When done most incorrectly, however, it can lead to children.)

When your Human correctly sleep with just itself, your mind will be at its emptiest, stupidest, and most easily tricked. It is during this time that you are susceptible to hallucinogenic trips through a self-created universe of gibberish called *dreaming*.

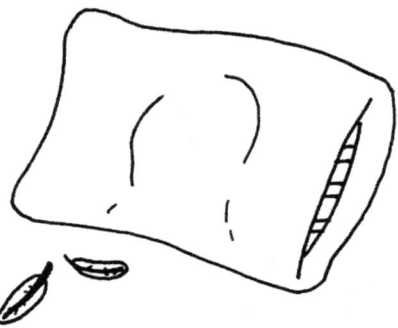

The main purpose of dreaming is to process all of the new information that your Human has received in the day, to keep some, to lose some, and to use what is left to unconsciously decide what kind of person you would like to be when you wake up tomorrow. Despite this, most people choose to be the same person everyday. While this choice might seem initially disappointing - considering all of the kinds of person they could choose to be - it actually makes sense because they already own the right clothes.

You will often completely forget your Human's nonsensical dreams, helping you to retain some continuity with the sensible, logical creature that you believe you are during the day.

Speaking of 'day,' most sleeping takes place at night, because less things happen at night, because everybody is asleep.

How to Get Up

'Getting up' in the morning is the most difficult thing any Human has to do before breakfast. Every day, the Human mind must wrestle the following three crises of willpower in order to get up:

I. CLARIFY REASONING

Beds are generally the safest place for your Human to be, so you should never risk getting up unless there are definitely going to be negative consequences otherwise. *Do you have a job? Is a lion approaching? Is your ongoing lack of any physical movement causing your body to become slow, useless and fatally paste-like?*

II. ACCEPT REALITY

What you were previously dreaming is likely to affect your mood when you wake up, so it is important to take a little time to re-adjust to reality. For example, if you've just spent the last few hours twitching enthusiastically because you believed you were *The Flying Ninja King of Dragon World*, it might suddenly seem a bit disappointing to be watching water boil while you stare sadly at an egg.

On the other hand, if you were having a horrible nightmare involving all your teeth turning into old, disintegrating carpet, it can be joyous to wake up to the usual, twinkling morning sounds of birds and binmen spitting.

III. ACTUALLY GET UP

Humans have two mysterious settings: *not being up*, which is characterised by wondering how you will ever get up; and *being up*, which is characterised by wondering how you got up. The quickest way for you to optimise a transition between these two bodily positions is to set a trap for yourself before you go to bed. This is most easily achieved by putting an alarm clock on the other side of the room the night before, or hiding it in a confusing pile of alarm clocks, or strapping it to the back of a large, easily panicked bird.

Eating

Your Human is a meat machine that needs fuel to power it. This means you must eat *food*, which is energy in its tastiest form. Luckily, almost all plants and animals contain a certain amount of energy, so your Human can eat most things that move or grow, just as long as those things are softer than your teeth.

Being able to eat every other kind of animal is a uniquely Human privilege, enabled mostly through the sneaky cleverness of tools. However, while Humans generally consider it quite an incredible achievement that they have wrestled themselves to the top of the food chain, it is still rare to see them bragging about it directly in the face of a lion or crocodile.

Food is crucial to operating Humans, so their highest priority remains the next thing they are going to eat. Human life therefore revolves around availability of food, which is why farms - where growing food is dirty, difficult work - are less popular than cities - where absurd amounts of clean, easy food constantly, magically exist in the shop at the end of your road.

Without exception, Human beings are always on the way from their last meal towards their next one, and simply try to keep civilisation going along the way. Society, economics, and politics might all seem like delicate mechanisms which must be maintained like a lot of spinning plates, but it's still important that all of those plates are empty first. It is harder to regulate an economy after all, if it is covered in jelly and old buns.

Indeed, everything impressive that Humans have ever achieved has been squeezed into the gaps between meal-times. Before you can have engineering and commerce and scuba diving, you must first have breakfast. This is why it is considered to be the most important meal of the day, because it almost inevitably leads to Mozart and space rockets.

Indeed, food is so important for mankind, it is often said that 'society is only ever three meals away from anarchy.' There is no point having institutions and leaders, after all, if they can't figure out between them how to make you a sandwich.

Helpful Tips

---

1   It is a very popular practice amongst Humans to *cook* their food. People like things hot, because hot things go cold, which injects drama and adds a thrilling deadline to the whole event.

---

2   Bland food is highly unfashionable. Luckily even the dullest meal can be made exciting by under-cooking it, using live eels instead of cutlery, or trying to eat the meal from a plate that is constantly accelerating because it has just been hurled from a cliff.

---

3   Your Human requires a wide variety of nutrients and minerals to function optimally. An 'unbalanced diet,' is so called because it leads your Human to becoming pear-shaped, wobbly, and generally more prone to sudden attacks of gravity.

---

4   Thin Humans are not necessarily healthy Humans. This means, a Human's diet should not primarily be judged on how far away their skin is from their skeleton, but when the contents between their skin and their skeleton are majority pie and cake material.

Meals

You are likely prefer to eat your Human's food in quick bursts called *meals*, to make the crude energy transfer process as creative, romantic and whimsical as possible This can be done by mixing shapes, colours, flavours, temperatures, and textures of different foods in charmingly defiant opposition to it all becoming the exact same mush in one hour. Because of jobs and sunlight, meal times now have a fairly standardised format across the world. Most Humans eat in the following three main stages:

I. BREAKFAST

Breakfast should be simple, and contain no more than two ingredients, preferably with one just poured on top of the other. Some people like breakfast in bed. Most people, however, prefer it in bowls or on plates.

Brunch, meanwhile, is a bourgeois, artistic form of breakfast reserved for people who are too free-spirited for a dogmatic breakfast regime, but not quite anti-establishment or impoverished enough to go straight to lunch.

II. LUNCH

Lunch is eaten during the middle of the day, which means you will have to stop whatever your Human is doing to eat it. This is why larger workplaces often have cafeterias. It's better not to lose an entire afternoon of industrial productivity because 9000 employees share a kitchen, and 8999 refuse to use the sink because bloody Dave has left his cup in there *AGAIN*.

In warmer climates with more relaxed cultures, lunch can be followed by a nap. In the warmest climates with the most relaxed cultures, this nap is then followed by a round of drinks, a nap, a street party, a national holiday, a month-long celebration of San Siestos (the patron saint of napping), a nap, a revolution, a nap, and then a brief hibernation period ending roughly in time for the annual Christmas party.

III. DINNER

Dinner is the meal that is normally eaten in the evening as a celebration that school, work or the most shameful portion of unemployment are over. As the 'party meal,' it is the mostly likely to be hot, exciting, dramatic, full of ingredients, split itnto courses, eaten with friends and relatives, and accompanied by alcohol or an argument.

Dinner should not be eaten too early, otherwise there is a danger that you will get hungry again before its time to go to sleep, and have to make another dinner. Likewise, dinner should not be eaten too late, otherwise there is a danger that you will fall asleep in it, and have to make another dinner, because you've ruined the previous one with your face.

WARNING: SNACKS

A 'snack' is officially defined by Human portioning experts as any piece of food that is smaller than their fingers, but bigger than the gaps between them.

The eating of snacks, or 'snacking,' is often considered risky survival behaviour in small tribes, as it is generally unauthorised by the very important people in charge of meals. You should avoid upsetting or undermining any person that is kind enough to feed your Human.

Snacks should therefore only ever be eaten out of boredom and never necessity, meaning it is important that they do not contain anything of significant nutritional value which could throw the body off-balance between sanctioned meals.

Chocolate, biscuits and crisps are therefore encouraged. Fruit, seeds, and nuts, meanwhile, should be strongly mistrusted, unless they form a completely unavoidable part of a cake.

Diets

Diet	Description
OMNIVOROUS	Carnivores come in two types: those who could personally hunt, kill, skin, gut and eat animals in the wild, and those who couldn't. The first type are the reason that meat exists, and the second type are essentially vegetarians. The only difference between the second type and other vegetarians is that they still will eat all animals, just as long as those animals no longer come in a directly recognisable animal shape.
FUSSY	Fussy eaters are people who don't eat a wide range of food stuffs, making them troublesome to cook for. They can also be annoying to go out for dinner with, assuming their fussiness is whiney, consistent and loud enough to divert your party away from a world famous steak house, and to a boiled potato restaurant of their choice.
VEGETARIAN	Vegetarians only eat the same food that animals eat, unless that food is an animal. Vegetarians are often people who have made a conscious choice to not eat everything they can, regardless of its flavour, which means their brains are smart enough to override their stomachs. Most vegetarians still eat fish, however, assuming that the fish didn't just swallow a cow.
VEGAN	Vegans do not eat anything that could cause a living creature distress, such as milk, cheese, eggs, or fireworks. Not wanting to cause animals distress sometimes puts vegans in a difficult position at dinner parties, because Humans are animals, and many Humans are distressed by vegans coming to their dinner party.

WARNING: DRINKING

According to Professor Nonsense from the University of Confused and Threatening Exaggeration, Human bodies are made up of 400% water, all of which must be replenished every day. Or else.

In general, a good rule of thumb is to drink any liquid that gets close enough to your Human's mouth to effortlessly fall in. There are, however, two note-worthy exceptions where some extra caution is advised: the first is a black coloured liquid called *coffee*; the second is an invisible coloured liquid called *alcohol*.

While both liquids still fulfil the basic Human need to constantly wet themselves inside themselves, these drinks also have noticeable side-effects when not consumed in moderation.

The side-effects of coffee are a combination of twitching, yawning, panicking, and productivity in various sequences, mostly depending on the time of day and the proximity of the next deadline. The side-effects of alcohol include confidence, wobbling, weeing, fun, and consequences.

Waste

After taking all of the useful stuff from your food and drink, your Human's body will need to get rid of any leftovers through several ridiculous waste removal processes. These are called *weeing* and *pooing*.

While these are essentially automated functions controlled by gravity, some valves on the lower half of the body must be mastered once your Human has stopped being a complete baby. This early muscle training is designed to give you ample time to purposefully relocate from wherever it is you are, to a specially-engineered and relaxing area that has been pre-designed for you to do the business. This area is called *nature*.

However, as nature increasingly decides to exist further and further away from people's natural habitat of cities, Humans have been forced to build a more convenient network of special portals to it called *toilets*. This elaborate system of chairs, holes, and hidden, horrifying tubes will help connect your Human's bum-hole directly to rivers and the sea.

Of course, waste can still be removed directly into rivers and the sea, although this nostalgic approach is increasing unpopular due to sharks, inconvenience, cold, and judgement.

Helpful Tips

1	Stick to popular, recommended toilet-using positions, like squatting and sitting. Please trust your long line of ancestors that these methods have been tried, tested, honed and refined over many millennia of trial and error, and proven to be the optimal positions for removing waste.
2	You should get into the habit of making progress towards the nearest waste disposal area as soon as your body first warns you. Not reaching the toilet in time is considered to be an unhelpful personality trait, and may even deter venture capitalists from investing in your brand.
3	There is no point washing and re-using toilet roll to try and save money, as it will lose about 99.8% of its structural integrity. Meanwhile, you will lose about 100% of your reputational integrity if witnessed.

Maintenance
Manual shape regulation

Exercise

Like a stone in a river, your Human may have a natural tendency towards roundness as you float through time. This is mostly due to the two most prominent, inbuilt survival mechanisms that nature has given you: *greed*, which wants you to go out on crazed, lustful sugar binges, and *laziness*, which wants you to lay around on sofas afterwards, letting that sugar settle into doughy layers of cuddle padding.

In order for your Human to function optimally, then, you should try to manually override these powerful instincts by regularly pestering and jiggling yourself through some sequence of repetitious movements. This is called *exercise*, and it is incredibly unpopular.

This is mostly because of a great contradiction at the heart of proper exercise: supposedly, exercise is intended to make you feel healthier, look better, and live longer. When done most correctly, however, you are more likely to feel dreadful, look disgusting, and believe you're probably going to die any second from a burst heart. When you bring up this contradiction - normally to a less sweaty person than you who is wearing a vest - they explain that you are supposed to feel horrible, so you won't feel so horrible next time, so you can do it for longer next time, so you'll feel less horrible until you feel horrible, then it won't feel so horrible until it feels horrible the next time and every time after.

This is the frightening logic of a jogger.

Of course, when more rational people are confronted with this idea - the prospect of *endless horrible* - they will instead respond, "Erm. Well. Actually, no thanks, I think I'd rather just sit here, look at my shoe-laces, and eat this deep-fried, meat-covered egg. Good luck with your bum-bag, big legs, and life. Good day, you lunatic."

In response, the less sweaty, vest-wearing people have tried to improve the experience of exercise over the years by making it fun and competitive. They added points, sticks, holes, lines, nets, teams, whistles, egos, violence, money, adverts, betting, cheating, and endless amounts of balls.

This innovation was called *sport*, and it worked out great for a while. Not only did it give exercise the kind of aggressive, tribal warfare dynamic it was obviously missing, but it also gave Humans a fun, new framework of rules which they could follow, use to compete, and/or freely misinterpret any time they wanted a nice opportunity to shout at a referee.

This was until the vast majority of Humans realised they didn't need to participate in the sport directly to enjoy it, but could instead have just as much fun watching other people do it from a great distance, while they sit down, drink beer, eat salted pork lumps, and shout.

Despite this, avid sports fans still burn off several calories a year, mostly by exercising their exhaustingly correct opinions in the direction of radios, televisions, and the most professionally-advised athletes in the world.

Types of Exercise

PREPARATION

Before any exercise is attempted, you must first 'warm' your Human 'up.' This involves pre-heating your muscles by lunging, thrusting, stretching and squatting in any way you can think of, as long as it looks ridiculous or entirely inappropriate within one kilometre of a playground.

Essentially, your Human should look from a distance like you are dancing the alphabet, except that it is your first day on Earth, you've never seen dancing or an alphabet, you are unsure of what you're trying to achieve, yet none of these facts have dampened your enthusiasm for the task.

WALKING

To move your Human from place to place, you must very quickly learn to move all of your weight in a confident falling-over direction by alternating which leg it is travelling over. It's staggering. When done properly, though, it's called *walking*.

Though it has become increasingly unfashionable, walking is still an essential Human skill for reaching the large metal containers which transport them, stalking dogs through parks, and getting to-and-from the pub. The latter is many models of Human's favourite kind of walking, so they will often try to prolong it in a number of creative ways. Popular methods include: spontaneously taking steps in the wrong direction, getting lost, wobbling, stopping to talk to people, stopping to talk to lampposts that look like people, and forgetting that they've left their keys in the pub. The latter is best realised at the very late point that they are already almost home, and are presently failing to open someone else's front door with their thumb.

Some people also walk purely for recreation, although these people are generally distrusted because of the sober yet conclusionless nature of their movements.

JOGGING

Jogging is popular, because it is a very obvious way to show people that you are a Human that exercises. If you want to keep your jogging a secret, however, you should not wear 'jogging clothes' at all, but simply incorporate small bursts of nonchalant jogging into your every day routine, by being late for work, impatient with public transport, and purposefully mistiming your toilet visits.

RUNNING

Running was invented shortly after jogging, presumably because someone jogged directly on top of a snake and their priorities suddenly changed. Running is now enjoyed by a wide variety of people, from runners, to muggers, to joggers about to be mugged by jogging muggers who are too competitive to accept their fate.

SWIMMING

Being a land mammal, if your Human has to swim, it is possible that something has gone quite wrong with your day. That is, of course, unless you voluntarily initiated the swim in a pool yourself, in which case it is just a wet, flappy form of exercise, mostly done in a lot of water, but also in at least a little bit of urine.

Homoeopaths agree with doctors that swimming is good for your Human. This is not because it is a low-impact cardiovascular exercise, however, but because the large amounts of water involved make it likely that every swimming pool contains at least one heavily-diluted cure for something.

GYMS

Gyms are places for people who want to walk, run, row, and cycle, but not go anywhere. The main problem with gyms, therefore, is that you have to go somewhere to get to one. This has led most people to conclude that by the time you have to go to one, you no longer need to go to one, so you might as well just stay home and eat a whole cooked chicken on a stick.

WARNING: GYMS

Joining a fitness studio is not a decision to be taken lightly. Indeed, using a gym without expert instruction and proper training can pose serious risks to your personality.

Indeed, the most dangerous misuse of gym equipment can lead to tragic cases of *Gym Personality Syndrome* (GPS), the symptoms of which include vanity, egotism, narcissism, boringness, and strongly impaired judgement about when it is appropriate to wear a vest.

Humans suffering from GPS can be found in almost all gyms, mostly by the full-length mirrors, confusing the person they see in those mirrors with a person that other people in the gym care about. Please remember, while gyms might well be public spaces, this does not necessarily mean that The Public has come only to watch you do enthusiastic and horrible squat thrusts in their general direction.

Basic precautions against GPS should begin at an early age, generally aiming to encourage 'fun' personalities, and/or discourage the kind that enjoy repetitive, thankless tasks in an indoor environment.

A healthy and well-adjusted adult, meanwhile, should only go to the gym *begrudgingly*, understanding it as nothing more than a cruelly necessary counter-balance to an excellent lifestyle of sugar, booze, and sitting down.

Trouble-Shooting

> **PROBLEM: MY HUMAN IS NOT PERFORMING AS FAST AS IT USED TO**

Is your Human being physically obstructed?

Common obstructions include ill-fitting trousers, being under water, being under water whilst caught in a net, and toddlers clinging desperately to your legs because they absolutely love you.

Is your Human correctly configured?

Humans have many different moving parts and hinges, all of which are just one wrong sneeze away from jumping out of place and causing their whole body to lumber around like a fabulous giraffe in a headwind. It is best to check that these moving parts are correctly aligned and assembled before attempting anything more complicated than a hiccup.

Is there any reason your Human should have low energy?

Humans are powered by bread, pasta, rice and potatoes, so you should check that your Human has been recently topped up with carbs. If your Human hasn't eaten for a longer period than usual, it is possible that its remaining energy has been diverted from its limbs, and towards its mouth area. This is to ensure crucial moaning processes are still operational.

Is your Human sufficiently motivated?

Humans often rebel against things they have to do, but don't want to do, by simply moving slower. This is called lolly-gagging, dilly-dallying, flim-flamming, boondoggling, shilly-shallying, frittering, dawdling, piddling, pottering, futzing around, goofing off, or faffing – but only by people who are so experienced in the procrastinatory arts that – like Eskimos in a world of snow - they can recognise every subtle, distinct shade of it.

Sometimes, this can be a simple coping mechanism to deal with the chore. More commonly though, it is a way to deal with the person who is making your Human do the chore, the general hope being that if you make doing the task so absolutely painful to watch, they will never ask you to do it again.

Is your Human sober?

Your Human can not always function at full speed and capacity when under the influence of alcohol. Decision-making can be slowed down by alcohol's effect on the brain; movement can be slowed down by alcohol's effect on the body; and ordering more alcohol at the bar can be slowed down by alcohol's effect on the bladder, crude navigational errors, and / or the inaccurate perception of the bar staff's interest in your drunken blibbering.

... or none of the above?

If you have done everything possible to optimise your Human, it is likely that any loss of performance quality is simply due to *ageing*. Ageing is quite natural, and happens all the time.

Despite this, some models of Human use something called 'anti-ageing cream' to try and combat the effects of time. It should be noted, however, that this is just a title given to the cream by the cream's manufacturers, and there is, as yet, no scientific evidence to prove that moisturiser has the ability to disrupt the linear sequencing of events.

You should not be discouraged if you feel your Human's increased years slowing you down, but should simply divert your ageing energy and resources to where they are most useful. Those who can no longer run marathons still have minds that have been alive for much longer than everyone else's, which means they should retain their superior abilities in the realms of nostalgia, historical context, and voting.

Optimisation
Configuration from Factory Settings

Washing & Cleaning

Looking after your Human's look and smell is an incredibly important part of the Human experience, especially for the people nearest to you that have to experience your Human.

While earlier models of Human were essentially self-cleaning because they lived directly in rain, wind, and flowers, more recent models must be cleaned regularly with *soap*. The regular washing and cleaning of your Human will keep it in good shape: looking healthy, smelling great, and tasting relatively neutral.

One of the most popular ways to wash your Human is to put it under a shower. It's also the quickest way to wash your clothes, shoes, and mobile phone, incidentally, assuming you have forgotten where your Human is standing while you are playing around distractedly with the taps.

Showers are most popular in places where time is considered to be an important commodity, because they are a predictable way to get wet without having to plan your day around rain. Despite this, important and busy people usually prefer to take baths. This is because 'showering' can suffer from all the usual loss of productivity associated with issues like:

- Having to stand up
- Having to balance
- Having to rotate like a weird kebab so water can land on all of your Human equally

In the meantime, your Human should be able to get a lot more done in the bath, because you can lay entirely still, but not all of your body has to be completely submerged in water.

Your head, for example, could stay dry, allowing you to answer the phone. Your hands could also stay dry, allowing you to hold the phone to your head, or simply drop it when you are ready to finish your call.

PICTURED: THIS BUSY HUMAN IS TAKING A QUICK 'POWER NAP'

Optimisation

Optional Maintenance

Some of your Human's other components will require some occassional attention in order to maintain your hard-won reputation as an impressive pillar of good-looking limbs and dazzling confidence. These are as follows:

Component	Maintainance Required
TEETH	Having a lot of teeth unfortunately means having a lot of gaps between teeth that smelly things can get stuck in. This is a problem because the mouth is hot, wet, and generally opens in the direction of other people's noses, making it an unappealing place to store a heroic strand of pickled cabbage for a week. Teeth should therefore be regularly bothered with a toothbrush. Children should brush their teeth in front of parents, so an adult can make sure they're doing it. Adults, meanwhile, should brush their teeth in front of a mirror, to make sure they themselves are doing it.
FINGERNAILS	Fingernails never stop growing, which is a highly risky attribute considering that they eventually become long, hard, unwieldy, sharp, spiralling, dangerous hand-swords. Luckily, most models of Human agree to regularly trim them, thus democratically avoiding a potential world of clumsy carpentry, ruined clothing, and nervous children who intuitively distrust the wisdom of crowds.
EARS	Ears collect wax inside them, which makes it harder and harder for them to hear what a bad idea that is. Unlike noses, which can be blown, and eyes, which can be cried,

ears must be manually cleaned with a pokey-shaped thing. Many Humans choose to use specialist cleaning implements like cotton-buds for this job, as wax often affects the usual deliciousness of fingers.

FACE

While it is impossible to completely change your face, your Human can sometimes adjust it slightly by using a collection of simple powders, paints and plasters. This is called *make-up*, and it is an easy, cost-effective and popular way to improve your face by painting a new face on top of your old one in a way that helps hide it.

HAIR

Functioning hairstyles need constant care, organisation, supervision and attention. Firstly, a style must be very carefully selected, or it will not visually broadcast your Human's intended tribal identity and values to other Humans who are seeking validation for that same set of values. Secondly, the hairstyle must be washed, or things will live in it.

Indeed, truly unwashed hair is likely to turn into *dreadlocks*, which is the hairstyle most likely to get caught in a fence. This is partly due to the inherent tangleyness of the hairstyle itself, of course, but also due to the attached lifestyle, which makes climbing over fences ideologically more attractive.

Alternatively, 'baldness' has become a very popular modern hairstyle, because it is quick, convenient, easy to wash, and goes well with bow-ties. It is also good for self-esteem, because it instantly replaces what scientists call "the area of the brain that subconsciously fears baldness" with a large, free mental space which you can focus entirely on filling with lovely, bald personality.

Getting Dressed

Almost all models of Human wear *clothes*. Those who don't are either considered incredibly normal or incredibly abnormal, depending mostly on whether they're in their native rainforest, or the customer service area of a bank in Frankfurt.

Clothes are worn for several main reasons:

- Protection from cold
- Protection from weather
- Protection from flappiest body parts from over-flapping

However, warmth and comfort are now considered bland requirements, and many brands of Human no longer get dressed only to compensate for their misplaced body hair. Indeed, while early models of Human would simply kill an animal, then climb inside it, in modern times things are a lot more complicated due to something called *fashion*.

Fashion is a kind of religion that many Humans follow, which means they have to dress in certain, specific ways, or risk alienation from their sect. Regardless of their specific beliefs, all dedicated followers of fashion must believe in *Cool*. While they will never see *Cool*, communicate with *Cool*, or have objective evidence that *Cool* lives anywhere outside their own heads, they must still have unshakeable faith in *Cool's* existence.

The important thing about believing in *Cool* is merely that you believe in the same *Cool* as the people around you, do not question *Cool*, and do what the high priests of *Cool* tell you to.

The priests of *Cool* are skinny people, often found in holy magazines looking serious, or on catwalk aisles looking even more serious, except wearing a dress they describe as *'glittered sunday robot* meets *urbanised frog revolution.'*

Clothes

T-shirts are pieces of fabric designed to cover the top half of your Human, featuring clever holes which allow you to continue using your head and arms in a way that is unimpeded by the cloth. Because they are the piece of clothing closest to the eye-line of children, it is not unusual for them to feature colours, opinions, and even helpful little logos which allow children to learn important lessons about the value of corporate branding.

Bras are, quite simply, fabric gravity-resistant boob hammock belts. They are worn almost exclusively by women to hold their breasts for them, despite many offers from men to help.

Shoes stop feet getting distracted by what kind of ground is beneath them. They are often made of a material that is harder than skin, making them a good thing to put between skin and the ground.

Socks cover the feet and function mainly as a lubricant for shoes. Socks are best when they can breathe. Socks are worst when the people around them can't. This happens regularly, precisely because socks spend their days between a hot, wet foot and a hard, tight shoe. Once socks are too smelly, they should be washed in pairs of three, as washing machines will always eat one as payment for their services.

Jewellery are bits of stone and metal which your Human can wear when you don't feel naturally sparkly enough. Decorating yourself with little shiny things that come from the ground is considered by most Humans to be an indication of good taste. While some jewellery is whimsical and detachable, the most precious kind should be stapled permanently on to the flappiest parts of the face and body through a process called *piercing*.

Hats come in different shapes for different purposes. Tall hats are the most impressive, wide hats are the most sun-resistant, small hats are the most enjoyable to point at, and electric hats are universally agreed to be the least appropriate during rainy weather. Hats are often the preferred method of insulating the head from cold, as they provide all the temperature benefits of large hairstyles, but are easier to remove in a cinema.

Underwear are the most commonly worn garment by Humans. Despite their prevalence in society suggesting they are extremely fashionable, Humans rarely wear them on the outside of their clothing where others would be able to see them. This makes other people's underwear an intriguing, alluring secret, which perhaps helps explain what drives adults into trying to see each others in any way they can.

Tattoos are jewellery made of ink and pictures, which are attached to the skin in a way that is not directly influenced by the forces of time, context or regret. Some tattoos are made up of only words, which offer many opportunities to communicate without talking. For example, Humans who have the words "love" and "hate" tattooed on their knuckles need only raise the appropriate fist when offered questions like, "how do you like the quiche, darling?", or, "are you sure you want a job in this nursery?"

Watches are wrist clocks that were invented because bracelets kept making people late, the idiots. Watches come in two types: *existent* and *non-existent*. When wearing a watch that exists, you can tell the time by looking at your Human's wrist. When wearing a watch that doesn't exist, you can tell the time by looking at your Human's wrist, then tapping it, then making a dumb face at someone who is wearing a watch that exists.

Trousers mostly come in the shape of legs. Some come in the shape of very small legs, but are worn by very big legs, giving off the impression that they are tight. This sounds simple enough, of course, but it's surprising how many Humans say things like, "wow, those trousers are too tight," despite it clearly not being the trousers' fault.

Belts are a way to tie trousers to the body so they do not fall down around the ankles in a way that would reduce movement or employability. Belts have holes in them, which is fine, because they're not pockets.

Suits are the official uniform of going to work, as they suitably, suitfully hide individuality and personality, making it easier for the world of banking and business to tick along without something pesky like humanity getting in the way. The only sanctioned way a suit can convey any vague personality is through the use of a wacky tie. Unfortunately, the wacky tie does not always convey 'wackiness' as desired, but more often 'tragic loss of perspective' and 'complete unbearableness.'

Pyjamas are clothes designed specifically for sleeping in, which means they are rarely worn in the day, or made from uncomfortable materials like denim, leather or aluminium.

Gloves keep Human hands either warm and clean, or warm and sweaty. Gloves are commonly worn during snowball fights, golf, and medical surgery, presumably because the lessened grip makes each activity more exciting for the person you're doing it with.

Glasses and sunglasses have become increasingly trendy, and are now worn by many people who are interested in cutting-edge style and fashion, especially because glasses often allow those people to see their own cutting-edge style and fashion in a less blurry way when confronted with a mirror. Sunglasses, meanwhile, are particularly helpful accessories for sunny days, because they effectively stop other people knowing where exactly you are looking, and sunny days are the times when all of the people you want to stare at creepily are looking their best.

Software
Culture: A Helpful Diagram

Core Motivations

While the potential applications for your Human are almost endless, there are nevertheless some shared core motivations which come pre-programmed into their source code, which often helps explain some of thei species more consistently silly behaviours:

SURVIVAL

One of the core motivations of all Humans is a desire to survive, both as an individual and, if it doesn't get too much in the way of the first goal, as a species. No matter how madly they claim to desire other things – whether they be cars, shoes, money, love, or their wallet – when you offer them a choice between the thing they proclaim to desire, or the chance to survive, most will immediately back-down and admit, "Erm, yeah, ok, I guess I would rather survive than keep my wallet, actually. You crack on, mate."

SECURITY

After they have mastered surviving, Humans then go after security, which is the maximising of comfort and minimising of risk, preferably at the same time. Security is also known as laziness, and it is one of the finest pleasures that a Human can experience because it is free, limitless, and you don't have to go anywhere to do it, making it immediately gratifying on a tight budget.

STATUS (AND MATING RIGHTS)

Status is an important, underlying part of Human culture, as it determines the potential order of the queue when more potential people need a potential thing than the amount of that potential thing exists. Humans are often trying to upgrade their status, and can collect all kinds of objects as 'status symbols.' From bigger houses to faster cars, there are many objects that are capable of speaking for a person, assuming that the thing the person can't say on their own is, "look at this thing. I don't need this thing, but I have this thing. It's my thing, and I win."

WARNING: SMOKING

Some models of Human also claim to need *nicotine* to function properly, especially after they start smoking, which is a surprising correlation, deserving of further study. Nicotine can be delivered into the bloodstream in a multitude of ways, but it is widely agreed that the "coolest" of these delivery systems is loads of cigarettes.

Unfortunately, the "coolness" of loads of cigarettes comes with a price-tag, which in this case is the physical unpleasantness one feels after many years of giving lots of money to the CEOs, board members and share-holders of tobacco corporations, who are almost all of the exact people in the world least like cowboys, rockstars, poets, artists, hedonists, and iconoclasts. In reality, every time a very, very cool person smokes a cigarette, a very, very uncool person somewhere gets enthusiastic about "what it has done to the graph."

In more recent times, e-cigarettes have grown in popularity as an alternative delivery system, providing all the same thrills of nicotine, yet with less of the surprising downsides of inhaling the crude combustion products of plants, glue and paper. In the future, health-conscious smokers hope to upgrade further, perhaps to voice-activated computer-chips in the brain. This way, when a nicotine craving pops up, they can simply shout 'CIGARETTE!' at themselves.

Smoking can also be bad for you in other ways, but luckily it is so easy to quit that most smokers manage to do it lots of times.

Heirachy of Needs

SUNSHINE / TOILET PAPER / LOVE / REGULAR GOSSIP

BIRTHDAY PARTIES / DREAMS / SHOES

SLEEP / JOKES / SECURITY

BEING RIGHT / FOOD

WATER / WIFI

FUN

Culture

Humans are pack animals, because it is a lot easier to survive, perform complex tasks and make jokes when there is more than one of you.

Indeed, back in caveman times, it was very difficult for a Human without a tribe to hunt, not be hunted, or get useful feedback on their punchlines. One of earliest recorded "jokes" that a tribeless loner of a cavemen drew on a cave wall, indeed, was a picture of a buffalo between two hands.

Not exactly hilarious, is it.

Perhaps even more important than a bad sense of humour for Humans, though, was how much harder it was to hunt without a pack. In a group, you could assign specialised roles, like scarer, chaser, catcher, holder, stabber, and project manager. The consequence of pack-hunting was that Human communities evolved to be completely reliant on each other, thus literally reliant on getting along. Being mean to people is a bad long-term strategy if you need those people to help kill an antelope.

Literally, whether your community liked or ostracised you became a life or death situation – there was nowhere else for you to go, and you couldn't survive alone – so Humans learned to be pretty friendly, pretty quickly. More than that, they learned to fear ostracism from their community above all else. Being disliked by people is an even worse long-term strategy if you want be invited to the antelope buffet at all.

Luckily, almost all Humans are born in a ready-made pack, so they only have to worry about staying in that particular pack. Generally, then, the best survival strategy is to be born, look at all the people closest to you, and then do the best impression of them that you can. If they're all wearing sauce-pans on their heads, and share the belief that any one not wearing a saucepan on their head is a dangerous traitor, then you know what you have to do if you want your share of dinner. Welcome to culture.

Helpful Tips

1	There are two kinds of Human in the world: *normal* and *weird*. 'Normal people' are easy to find, because they are like you. You know how normal you are? Well, they're like that too. 'Weird people,' however, are different, and should therefore be avoided until they stop that.
2	Human brains have natural, inbuilt limits to the number of people they can really care about and emphasise with. This causes *tribal bonding*, but also *societal detachment*. To find out your number, you simply need to arrange everyone you know into a big, long line, walk along it smiling, then stop counting when your face hurts.
3	Strangers are just friends you haven't met yet. Don't get too sentimental about this fact though. Afterall, friends are just strangers that you haven't forgotten yet due to an ice-skating head injury.

Operating Systems

Despite photographs from space seeming to prove that Earth has just one big, basically connected, dry, green bit, the majority of people on that one big, basically connected, dry, green bit still seem to prefer the conclusion that it is actually made up of around 200-300 entirely different and separate parts called 'countries', 'territories' and 'colonies', the number of which is decided internationally and unanimously by the last person to edit Wikipedia.

Depending on/in which of these sectors your Human was manufactured will determine the two main forms of *operating system* that your Human is most likely to run on:

COUNTRIES

When most models of Human are created, they are immediately registered with a friendly, neighbourhood corporation called a 'country'. Whichever corporation they are registered with as a baby is the one that owns them, gives them permission to leave or come back, and the one that they're later going to share their wages with.

Indeed, countries are neither 'a group of people' nor 'an area of land', but the limits to which one institution can tax a group of people in an area of land before another one takes over. To make this all a bit more exciting, countries often have their own songs, missiles, and netball teams.

Liking your own country remains a very popular thing to do, no matter what your country actually is or does. This is called *patriotism*, and it is common to every Human in every country, suggesting Humans don't so much love their particular country for what it is, but just love it because it contains them.

RELIGIONS

Despite life being a near-death experience, Humans often spend some of it trying to figure out their own answers to the age-old questions that have been with their species since the dawn of thumbs: "why is there stuff, what is the stuff, and why did whatever the stuff is need me here to look at it?" These people are called *philosophers* and *scientists*.

However, if you don't want to waste your entire life looking at tiny or massive dots through a microscope or telescope, or trying to figure out what "is" *is*, then luckily you can just ask your friendly, neighbourhood *religion* instead. To get started, simply look around around your immediate vicinity for the person wearing the most impressive hat.

Essentially, religions are a diverse set of rules and rumours, which can be enjoyed by any Human with an infinite amount of curiosity, but only a finite amount of life.

Language

Before there was a language, it is widely accepted that there wasn't one. If there was, at least, nobody talked about it.

This means that early models of Human were forced to communicate by making angry grunts, hungry grunts, confused grunts, suggestive grunts, and through quite a bit of horny winking. Then, one slow day, a particularly bewildered-looking savage pointed a poo-knuckled finger at the big yellow warm thing in the sky, and went, 'EURGH.'

The Human next to him agreed.

When the big yellow warm thing eventually went away again, someone else cautiously suggested, 'AURGH?'

This noise was greeted less enthusiastically. Indeed, there was some debate about the similarity of the second noise to the first noise, but luckily this debate didn't last very long because of the amount of noises that were currently available to debate with.

Eventually, these grunts started to become recognisable, familiar sounds that represented consistent ideas. In this case, *big yellow warm thing come*, and, *big yellow warm thing go away*. These verbal symbols could then be shared within the Human tribe and passed down the generations.

Once they'd nailed the concept of *words*, it wasn't long before models of Human everywhere were pointing fingers and making noises at *trees* and *women* and *feet* and *spiders* and *noises* and *make* and *kinds* and *sentences*, and were using those noises to make all kinds of sentences.

This was a clever development, as it allowed communication – a way to swap knowledge, retain it over time, and use it to complete group tasks with minimal confusion. Gone were the days of communication mishaps where two models of Human talked about how they were going to kill an antelope together, and then one of them accidentally went in the wrong direction and built a wardrobe.

Unfortunately for recent models of Human, much of the initial cleverness of developing language has been lost, as it soonafter began to follow the wonky and annoyingly directionless path of natural selection. It expanded. It adapted. Sometimes new words would emerge; some times old words would die out. Smart innovations evolved, but lots of dumb nonsense survived. Most frustratingly, it wasn't long before it started splitting off into different language families, which would eventually become completely unrecognisable to each other. 廢話! Exactly.

Many thousands of years later, international relations and diplomatic politics are still presumably relying on a similar system of angry grunts, hungry grunts, confused grunts, suggestive grunts, and through quite a bit of horny winking, which is why they haven't yet progressed past the "us/them" phase of friendly planetary sharing.

Helpful Tips

1	Your Human's brain is very clever, and can even perform unasked for tricks that let you you understand somehtnig even when some words are repaeted or even scrmabled up.
2	FACT: If you didn't know a language, you wouldn't understand this.

Emotions

While possessing the kind of brain that could theoretically invent a yo-yo, your Human is not naturally gifted as a rational thinker. This is because they simultaneously possess the kind of brain that *could* invent invent the yo-yo, but also the kind of brain that *would* invent the yo-yo.

Your Human also has no innate understanding of statistics or probability, which might cause you to have all kinds of irrational reactions to normal problems. For example, if you asked a Human, "how many people need to be in a room, so that the probability that two of those people share a birthday reaches 50%?" They would not intuitively know. Furthermore, despite the answer obviously being 23, it is likely that the Human would spend so long trying to work it out on their fingers and toes that they would forget to buy any presents. Humans are easily confused.

You may also regularly forget that the universe is completely indifferent to your Human, and continue to believe you are things like "lucky" or "unlucky." These reactions are essentially glitches in the body-brain connection that cause behaviour to deviate away from nature's general narrative of cold, uncaring logic, and towards something that is more entertaining to watch on TV. These subjectivity-powered sanity wobbles are called *emotions*.

You are likely to have a negative reaction when your Human loses money. This emotion is called *suffering*. You are likely to have a positive reaction when your Human finds money. This emotion is called *happiness*. The fact that you can have both of these reactions towards the exact same bit of money, just several minutes apart, is either good evidence of how completely insane your default settings are, or better evidence that you should sew up the holes in your Human's pockets.

However, this is not what makes your Human so special, as most models of animal also have these two emotions, although in a decidedly less glamorous form. If animals could use Human language, these emotions would be called "Hey! Great! Grass!" and "OH NO I'M IN A SCARY MOUTH HELP."

No, the thing that separates your Human from other models of animal is the massive spectrum of weird, inventive and non-essential emotions they can experience in between, all courtesy of their massive, constant success as life-forms.

Common Emotions

Fear comes from definitely knowing there is going to be a future, and yet knowing absolutely nothing about whether it will contain clowns. While some fears are irrational, like the fear of ducks being a bit too near patterned umbrellas, most fears evolved to protect us from a real and possible threat. The almost universal fear of darkness and strange noises, for example, evolved to warn early models of Human in the grassy wilderness about the possibility of nearby clowns.

Happiness is caused by expecting things to be bad, and then those things not being as bad as you expected, probably because of chocolate. Happiness is always temporary, which is what makes it such a nice thing to want. Actually attaining permanent happiness would, of course, be disastrous, except for people selling self-help books called 'The Happiness Delusion: How to Regain Your Sadness.'

Regrets are a way for Humans to torture themselves by imagining a parallel universe where they are not as clumsy, stupid, or irresponsible as they are in the one they actually inhabit. In this imaginary realm, there are no consequences, just endless delightful arguments and situations where every single thing you do and say is entirely correct, spectacular, and fully witty. Regrets only exist in this universe because time machines don't.

Boredom is the one of the most common Human emotions, as it is caused by nothing novel happening for several seconds. There is an almost limitless amount of potential boredom to be had in the world, which is what makes it one of the main driving forces in society. Without boredom, there could be no adventures, fun, or laughter, because there would be no incentive to create it.

Confusion is one of the least understood of all the emotions because it can strike even the smartest model of Human at galactic haircut trouser nuisance.

Excitement is closely related to the concepts of *time* and *presents*. It is most common in children, because they have less anecdotal experience of its inevitable relationship with disappointment. Excitement makes some people so bad at waiting that they actively try to make time pass more quickly. Unfortunately for them, this is entirely illegal due to the International Law of Clocks.

Anger is an exciting form of hope. It normally occurs when a thing is not quite as good a thing as you thought that thing could be, making you want to scream at that thing until it changes. It's essentially optimism, in its shoutiest form. The most productive Humans are therefore the ones who only get angry at things that they can actually change. Conversely, the least productive people are the ones who are more likely to drop a cup, then spend four hours loudly reprimanding gravity.

Love is an involuntary response to awesomeness. Humans are always trying to "find love," which is a doomed idea, because it is stealthy and almost entirely invisible. It is therefore much smarter to help love *find you*, by either being born incredibly rich and good-looking, or, alternatively, by always trying to become a much more loveable person. Your aim should be to be such a great person, indeed, that you can simply stay on the sofa in your pants, leave the door open, and wait for 'The One' to wander in by accident.

Jealousy is an unhelpful feeling, most commonly associated with not being the absolute best person in the entire world. Envy can be a particular problem in romantic relationships, though the relationships that last the longest are those that have learned to alleviate jealousy with the regular application of trust and/or cages.

Sadness is mostly caused by positive assumptions. To avoid it, you should wake up and immediately imagine that your Human's upcoming day will be a grand spectacle of constant failure, avoidable accidents, miserable conversations, clumsy walking, wrong food, bad manners, and ants. Only after this kind of rational pessimism can an ordinary, boring, uneventful Tuesday be celebrated like it's an Olympic victory of epic proportions.

Confidence is an emotion that makes a Human feel like nothing is going wrong, irrespective of how wrong it is actually going. People who do well in Human society, then, are generally that society's most confident people. This does not mean they are the people who are the best at what they do, of course, but simply that they have so much confidence that their belief in themselves is never affected by something as trivial as reality.

Loneliness is the feeling that Humans most try to avoid. However, you can not avoid loneliness, or hide from it, or run away from it, since there is only ever going to be you in your own head, and that's where your whole life is going to take place, even if you keep putting that head in lots of different places. It is therefore best to try and befriend your loneliness. Great places to befriend your loneliness are libraries, submarines, and your shed.

Disgust mostly exists to prevent you from eating things your Human shouldn't, thus protecting you from bacteria, illness and social judgement. In this way, Disgust is your Human's friend. It's just not a very cool friend. Indeed, it's more like the kind of friend you inherited from your parents and are still obligated to hang out with, even though you'd much rather be spending play-time with cooler kids like Curiosity, Adventure and Recklessness. Still, any time your Human has a strong feeling of disgust, you should be pleased to know that the feeling is probably preventing you from doing something stupid, like curiously, adventurously, recklessly licking the thing you're disgusted by.

Embarrassment is a feeling that has been with Humans since antiquity. It is characterised by an intense discomfort with oneself, not when one does something stupid, but when one does something stupid and someone else notices. The most common and universal causes of embarrassment are: failed high-fives, failed hand-shakes, constant sweaty fart noise sex, and failing to hide a stumble behind a sudden bit of weird jogging.

Hope is the soundtrack of the Human condition, and it happens when you want something, but don't think your Human has the power to influence the getting of it. Your Human can hope for many things - from sunny days, to on-time departures, to world peace - the key point being that trying to change any of them would require enormous amounts of skill, planning, magic, or work, whereas hoping for them sounds just as nice and can still be achieved from a hammock.

WARNING: EMOTIONS

In order to keep your Human sane and healthy, it is important to express your emotions, and not 'bottle them up.'

While emotions are generally bothersome - and it might seem like a relatively quicker and easier fix to just ignore them until they go away - it is more likely that keeping in your feelings will cause you further problems instead, as they rattle around your brain like old eggs in a washing machine.

This is particularly important in relationships, when your unexpressed concerns continuously store up into ever bigger and wronger mind lists, only to be expressed one day, all at once, out of context, at an unhelpful volume, in a provocative way, on a long car journey, at speeds rarely conducive to jumping out the window.

Despite the apparent difficulties, you are generally advised to express your emotions whenever your Human feels one. It is therefore important not to get *your emotions* mixed up with *your opinions*, which should definitely be bottled up for a very, very long time, then mulled over, then revisited, then re-examined, then checked, then re-checked, then copied on to a new piece of paper, then proof-read, then put back inside the bottle, and then thrown into the sea so every one can get on with their lives.

Applications

Your Human can be upgraded in a staggering number of ways, by simply installing new skills and knowledge.

Your Human has a sponge-like mind, and should be dipped in lots of different kinds of knowledge liquids. Alternatively, you could stay entirely in one liquid, until you drown yourself in your own expertise.

AVAILABLE UPGRADES:

MUSICAL ABILITY

Musical abilities increase sex appeal, mostly in proportion to the kind of instrument played. Generally, ones you play with your hands are more sexy than ones you have to blow very hard on with your face. This is mostly because they free up said face to look casually haunted by the burden of its own poetic genius.

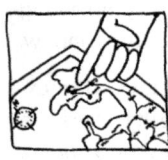

TRAVEL

Travelling is a quick way to become wiser, as interaction with different cultures allows you to see how absolutely weird and foreign your own one is. Travelling can be addictive, however, mostly due to it's massive similarity to what normal people call 'holidays.'

SWIMMING

Swimming is an essential Human skill, which should be learned by any one who doesn't want to spend an equal amount of time learning the alternate skills one can use when confronted with large amounts of water, such as extensive floating or breath-holding until rescue.

EDUCATION

Learning is a great way to broaden your conversational appeal by giving you more things to say than what your Human was born with. Learning a bit will make you feel smart. Learning a lot, however, will make you feel *wise*, which is the depressing point you become smart enough to realise how stupid you are.

FOREIGN LANGUAGE

Learning a second language allows Humans to talk behind each others' backs, although in front of each others' faces (this is, of course, assuming there are people in-between their faces and their backs which understand that second language also.) If your conversation partner doesn't understand your second language also, please remember that you're just being noisey and confusing.

DRIVING

As vehicles are extensively used your Human's society, learning to drive is a skill at least as useful as being able to ask for a lift. Your Human must be a certain age to learn to drive, so you can either reach the pedals or afford to pay for the crash when you can't.

HOBBY

A hobby is a passion that is pursued in your Human's time outside of work. As such, hobbies do not have to be personally useful, collectively understandable, or financially rewarding. This frees them up to be so entirely ridiculous that they can involve stamps or frisbees.

ARTISTIC TALENT

While art is celebrated as coming from a deep, mysterious part of the Human's 'soul,' good art is mostly achieved by annoyed people doing the same kinds of thing in the same kinds of ways, over and over again, with very little success or reward. It is best when practised monotonously like a boring, weirdo machine.

COOKING

Cooking allows you to eat a much wider range of ingredients by learning how to combine them in ways that taste good and don't kill you. Humans have to learn to cook by experimenting, then eating. The smartest chefs therefore feed their experiments first to other people, until they've been proven safe enough for their creator (normally about 40 minutes later.)

MARTIAL ARTS

You can feel more secure and confident in your day-to-day life by learning to throw your Human's hardest bits at other people's softest bits. This is called *self-defence*, and it should not be misused to defend things other than the self, such as reputations, relationships, or the ownership of a cinema arm-rest.

Operation
Improving Native Functionality

Major Hazards

Your Human can be used in many contexts, situations and exciting environments, but it's operational integrity may be impaired by the following hazards:

DROWNING

While your Human is relatively water-proof, you should not leave yourself under the surface of any liquid for more than a long breath if you want to retain the majority of your aliveness. Humans can drown in even small amounts of liquid, which is why cups are generally designed to be smaller than their heads.

FIRE

Human hair is flammable, and should therefore be kept away from naked flames at all times that you don't desperately need the attention of a fireman. Should you inadvertently catch fire, you should *stop*, (regret what you've done), *drop*, and *roll*, preferably into a fire station, where qualified personal can then do their best to advise you on how to further proceed with the incident.

NATURE

Your Human should not be left in the wilderness for long periods of time because nature contains spiders, holes, pointy things, scary things, and weather. Humans, meanwhile, have lost their native ability to survive the causal madness of nature for more than about six minutes without cheating with tools.

ITSELF

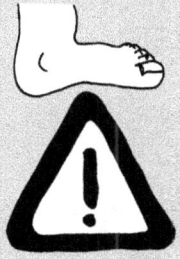

By far the biggest danger to your Human is *itself*, the threat of which you can always identify by walking up to a mirror, looking at it, and then jiggling about a bit. Clearly, any creature with a native capacity for boredom, ignorance, curiosity and creativity should not be left alone for long periods of time without supervision. For a bored, unsupervised Human, every dumb new idea involving back-flips or power tools is an exciting adventure in irresistible consequences.

Jobs

Most models of Human have something called a *job*, which is where they go in the day so they can afford somewhere to go at night.

While previously every model of Human had only one type of job (a position titled 'Human'), now there are so many things that need doing, jobs come in an almost endless range of intricately specialised types. No longer can your Human just build a table. No. Now your Human must manage the supervisor of the inspector checking the quality of the table's leg screw manufacturer's robot.

Essentially, then, a job is just a trade-off between two commodities: *time* and *money*. If you've got time, you can swap that time for a little money. If you've got money, you don't need a job, effectively buying yourself a lot of time. Meanwhile, if you only want to swap a little bit of your time for a lot of other people's money, you should look for a job in either crime or banking, depending mostly on whether or not you want to sit on a chair.

Different kinds of job are often paid vastly different salaries. This is rarely based on how hard or essential the jobs are, incidentally, but mostly on how many of that job exist, and how many people are available that can do those jobs.

This system is called *supply and demand*. While it is a sometimes useful method of distributing labour, it also tends to cause some embarrassing discrepancies, as summarised in this table:

JOB	AMOUNT EARNED	WHAT THEY DO
Workers	A little	Work
Landlords	A lot	Exist

Humans often say, "jobs don't go on trees." This is a very basic fact of reality that only gets more obvious as you accurately understand what a job and a tree are. However, because jobs do not go on trees – indeed, because jobs absolutely *can not* grow on trees, so dissimilar are they as concepts – Humans instead have to look for them, find them, acquire them, and try to keep them. This process, which is fun for the kind of people who are the opposite of fun, works as follows:

CHOOSING A JOB

Choosing a job is about figuring out what skills you have, and where you can apply those skills for the most potential gain. Don't worry if you don't have any skills, however, as almost every company has at least a few positions available for people with absolutely no skills whatsoever. These are called *management* and *consultancy* positions.

CAREERS ADVICE

Careers advice services exist to help undecided people choose what jobs they could do.

However, if you think you might like to be a careers advisor, you should beware that most career advisors were advised by their career advisors not to advise any one to get a career in careers advice, just in case they end up advising themselves out of a career.

Indeed, you should be very suspicious of your careers advisor if they start randomly blurting out suggestions like 'plumber,' 'woman,' or 'curtain maker,' as it probably means they just don't want competition in the glamorous careers advice industry.

Alternatively, if they start telling you how fantastically rewarding careers advising is, while simultaneously admiring the hours and flexibility of your directionless unemployment, it might be possible to just swap chairs.

APPLYING FOR JOBS

Once you've figured out what your skills are, the next step is to find people who don't have those skills, and are willing to admit that embarrassing fact in public by paying you.

Jobs vacancies are normally advertised in newspapers, just before the obituaries. Smart job-seekers should therefore check both sections carefully before applying for any job, just in case the advertised 'Dog Walker' position is somehow related to the string of obituaries mentioning 'sudden, outrageously horrible dog bite death in the line of duty.'

Most models of Human apply for jobs by sending in a CV. Essentially, a CV is a long list of compliments given by oneself to oneself, in the hope that someone else will believe at least some of them. CVs should include your job history, favourite teacher, interesting skills that can be whipped out around the office on a slow day, and just enough information about what you do in your spare time to convince the prospective employer that you're not going to start sleeping in the office overnight.

PROMOTIONS

The more you work, the more your Human's skills are worth to a company. However, the more your Human works, the more your Human will inevitably want to quit, run away, and go chase butterflies in a field.

This is a problem for employers, which is why they invented *promotions* and *pay rises*. Promotions are a company's way to ensure Humans will keep not leaving them, in direct relation to how much those Humans increasingly will want to.

CHANGING JOBS

There are three ways to change job – *quitting*, being *made redundant*, and *getting fired*. Quitting is like getting fired, except you do it to yourself when you're unhappy with your company's performance. Being made redundant is like quitting, except arranged by other people on your behalf. Getting fired is like being made redundant by yourself, and is often preceded by doing something completely excellent like getting caught by your boss playing wheely-chair Olympics.

The way in which you leave a job is important information to tell, change, lie about, or hide from your next employer, depending on whether those circumstances make you more or less attractive as a prospective employee. For example, quitting because your skills were "not appreciated" at your previous employer sounds much better than being fired because your skills were "not noticed" by your previous employer, because you spent the majority of your day trying to climb inside the fax machine.

RETIREMENT

Retirement is the only kind of unemployment that you have to earn.

Unlike actual unemployment, being retired means you no longer have to make excuses or explain why you don't have, want, or need a job. This is because simply telling people you're "retired" instantly informs them that you've done a whole lifetime of work already, and are therefore able to enjoy insane and ridiculous hobbies completely free of their judgement.

Popular Jobs

An **academic** is a special kind of older student who accidentally studied something useless, then was forced to teach the same subject to other, younger students in order to pay back their embarrassing loans. This is called *academia*, or a pyramid scheme, depending on how academically qualified the person is you ask.

Scientists are people who never stop asking 'why?', and are therefore useless in any business that involves talking to customers. This is because "Why? Why? Why?," is quite a reasonable set of questions to ask atoms, nitrogen and the Universe, but quite an annoying response to many customer inquiries, such as "hello" or "what time do you close?"

Criminals are the very important people who sell all of the stuff that shops aren't allowed to. Criminals therefore tend to respect 'the law' a lot more than normal Humans, because it is what provides their jobs. Indeed, the more things the government makes illegal, the more employment opportunities there inevitably are in the lucrative crime sector of the economy. When politicians say things like "we are going to be tough on crime!", up-and-coming criminals hear, "we're hiring!"

Builders are people that put bricks on top of other bricks until there are enough bricks all in a row that they can have a tea break. Builders can often be seen outside buildings not doing anything. Of course, 'outside buildings' is the worst place to complain about what they're not doing, because, even if they aren't doing anything, they can point at the buildings they're outside of, and say, "who'd you think built those? Florists?"

Teachers have one of the most important jobs of all, as they teach Human children stuff they don't want to know. Luckily, teachers jobs are made much easier by the existence of *schools*, where children have to go if they want to make friends. Before schools existed, teachers had the much harder job of trying to hunt children down, catch them, and shout facts at them until they were adults.

Politicians are people whose jobs are to say things. Politicians come in two main types: the first are the kind that blame the other for not doing anything, and the other type are the ones not doing anything. Every few years, these two groups switch.

Cleaners are some of the most respected Humans in all of the world, not because they are cleaners, but because they allow so many millions of others to be messy-ers, which is fun. Cleaners are therefore wonderful, and should be regularly kissed on the head.

Doctors are people that have studied the Human's hardware, so know a lot more of the things that can go wrong with it than anyone else. However, despite their superior expertise, some models of Human still don't like visiting their doctor. This number would be considerably lower, however, if doctor's default advice was *to keep having the maximum amount of fun possible*, instead of being so adamant on spreading 'real advice' like "cut down on the morning vodkas and don't melt cheese on every meal." Doctors are generally well respected in society, except by vets, who see them as lazy cheaters for only learning one species.

Farmers are organic, free-range Humans that grow everybody's food in exchange for money and farmer jokes. Luckily, modern farmers are rarely bothered by these jokes, as they are almost exclusively made by Humans who live in tiny boxes in cities, and wouldn't know how to feed themselves if they weren't allowed to sit inside all day for tokens they can swap for it.

Police officers are in charge of catching just enough criminals to look useful, but not so many that they render themselves obsolete. Being too good at policing would be absolutely disastrous for the police. Being a police officer in a crime-free society, after all, would be like being a lifeguard in an abandoned biscuit factory.

Artist jobs are few and far between, because their popularity-to-usefulness ratio makes them very competitive. On the plus side, this means that there is only space in the art world for Humans with the most desire for attention. On the negative side, this means that there is only space in the art world for Humans with the most desire for attention. Incidentally, it is difficult to define exactly what an artist is, which is actually what makes it such a glamorous profession to people who, from the outside, don't seem to be doing much more than trying to express their boring thoughts and feelings for cash.

Professional Athletes are individuals who have mastered an incredible, exhausting skill to an elite standard. This skill is called *interviewing*. Many Humans believe that sportsmen and women are generally over-paid and over-celebrated, though this is because they don't understand the determination, dedication, and life-long perseverance it takes to finish a thousand identical sports games, then say to a camera, "yes, tough game, they tried to win, we tried to win, and obviously only one of us did. Incredible. Good night."

Carpenters make trees into different, smaller, more useful shapes like tables. Despite the more recent popularity of ceramic, metal and plastic, wood remains a very popular material for Humans to have around the house. This is because it profoundly reminds them of their roots; a time when they all lived in the trees, because those trees were their home, because those trees existed, because those trees weren't tables.

Celebrities are Humans which are famous for 'something'. How important that 'something' is has changed drastically over time. Indeed, once upon a time you became a celebrity for doing 'something', then people pointed cameras at you. Now it is the other way around.

Office jobs exist because Humans assume they can solve any problem by simply throwing paper, desks, and chairs at it. This is not true, and is often just a waste of perfectly good paper, desks, and chairs. This is why so many people choose to store those items in offices, because the risk of them becoming airborne is reduced considerably by the existence of walls and bosses.

Models have the nicest kind of job, where the hard work is generally over once you're been born with a vaguely symmetrical thing on top of their neck. As such, models are not given large amounts of responsibility in society, beyond getting dressed, standing still, or walking up and down in a straight line whilst looking bothered.

Astronauts are incredibly fussy Humans who literally don't want to do any job on earth. They are often punished by being put in a flying tin can and sent to Nothing to do Something.

Accountants are babysitters for people who have to use money, but who don't really understand money, mainly because money is frightening and formalised nonsense. Most accountants are able to count lots of numbers in a row and come to the correct total. Only the best accountants, however, are able to count all of the same numbers in a row, move those numbers somewhere else, and come up with a magical new total that defies the laws of maths yet somehow lets you buy a tax-free yacht.

Lawyers are the ultimate tools Humans can use to upset each other. Of course, there are good lawyers and bad lawyers, just like in any other profession. It is, however, much harder to tell the difference with lawyers because of how irrelevant it is to their jobs. Because they are only *interpreting the law* – whatever that says – lawyers don't need to be moral or immoral, only *amoral*. Generally speaking, having *a* moral pays better than having several morals.

Electricians are plumbers for light-bulbs. Humans should not become electricians if they are allergic to light, or clumsy, or colour-blind, or wet, or anti-progress.

Acting is the only job that involves pretending to do all other jobs. It is therefore one of the most celebrated careers in the real world with many regular, prestigious award ceremonies, because of the amount of pretend difference it makes in every conceivable area of pretend life.

Managers are Humans who used to do things, but are now employed to watch other Humans do things, and then give helpful feedback like "good job!" and "that's your final warning!"

Drunks are special kinds of alcoholics that don't regret their alcoholism in any way, but instead dutifully treat it like a job. They can normally be found around town, exactly where you would expect to find them, dedicated as they are to their strict drinking hours and their rigid time-tables of intermittent loitering near shops, bus stops, and park benches.

Musicians are people that hang around with drummers, in order to help disguise some of the noise they're making. The existence of musicians also means that drummers get to be part of something called a *band*, which is an exciting opportunity to turn hitting things with sticks into music.

Helpful Tips

1	Getting a job you are good at, enjoy, or that you find rewarding is highly motivational. Generally, you should be able to tell how much you like your job from how you feel when you're not doing it. If your 'spare time' is mostly filled with stress, fear, and dread about work, for example, it's possible you're not letting your heart be the pilot of your dreams.
2	If you feel like you are becoming unhappy in your profession, think about changing it to something entirely different, like a holiday.

WARNING: MONEY

Life as the latest model of Human is not so much about learning useful survival skills like feeding yourself and finding shelter, as these problems have been solved by people who were born first. Luckily, these people are more than happy to swap all of the land, food and property they "own" (their words) for something called *money*.

Money is made of buttons, dead trees, maths, and sadness. Luckily, it doesn't really exist, though most people agree to ignore its incredible non-existence for the sake of day-to-day convenience. Generally, the higher the number of your money, the happier you are. For example, most Humans agree that having 5620 money is better than having 33 money, which is better than having 4 money. (It should be noted that having zero money used to be the worst amount of money you could possibly have. This is until *debt* became trendy, at which point zero money became a very fashionable sign that you were 'bouncing back.')

Everyone has to *earn money* to *buy things*, but the things you have to buy should be a helpful indicator of roughly your position on the grand scale of society. If you have to *earn money* to *pay rent*, for example, you're probably near the bottom. If you're one of the people receiving that money, and using it to buy things like sofas, low calorie crackers, and trombone lessons, you're most likely nearer the middle. If you aren't sure what 'rent' exactly is, but are certainly intrigued enough by the concept to ask the butler once he has returned to your side of the castle, you're somewhere near the top. In which case, congratulations. *Champagne all round, Binky!*

Getting Around

The ultimate goal of your Human's society is to reach a stage - through technological, logistical, economic and spiritual progress - that actual face-to-face interaction with other Humans becomes an optional pursuit, and no one is forced to leave their house at all, unless they have some weird desire to remember a tree. *Outside* has only ever caused Humans problems, after all (tornadoes, winter, jellyfish, etc.)

Unfortunately, humanity has not yet reached this illustrious point, so they must still haul their bodies from place to place via one of the following transportation methods:

BICYCLES

Cycling is a way for your Human to walk whilst sitting down, go longer distances without paying for transport, and be environmentally friendly whilst directly inhaling car exhausts.

Luckily, bicycles are one of the most efficient machines on the planet for turning your Human's natural energy into forwards motion. Indeed, the only machine that is more energy-efficient is perhaps the horse-drawn bicycle, which requires only occasional verbal energy from your Human to encourage the horse.

Despite the many advantages, however, there are also dangers involved in bicycle riding. These include punctures, tight clothing, punctured tight clothing, falling off, and falling on when you've punctured your tight clothing, which is especially dangerous for the flappier parts of a gentleman

CARS

Cars are the preferred mode of transport for people who enjoy life's little luxuries because they are expensive to buy, maintain, repair, clean, insure, tax, fuel, drive, crash, park, rent, and scrap, but give you complete control of the radio on your journey.

Despite the costs, cars remain incredibly popular with Humans, with some busier models of Human owning as many as one each. It is, of course, harder to drive cars in cities because of the amount of cars that are already there. Most city drivers are aware of this, so drive as poorly as possible to in order to discourage further motorists from getting involved.

For some Humans, cars are preferable to taking public transport. Indeed, they are appealing *because* they are private transport, allowing you to drop someone off somewhere and stay inside the car, wearing only your ugly old pants. This is also true if you are picking someone up, of course, though in this case it is best to warn the person ahead of time that you will be wearing less clothing than an equivalent bus driver.

On many parts of Earth, Humans must be at least a certain age before they're allowed to drive. Before you learn to actually drive, however, you must first pass a driving test.

Essentially, this test involves driving around in a small car with a giant, flashing orange cone on top in an industrial car park in a way that would infuriate other motorists if you were doing it in a normal car on a normal road.

TAXIES

Taxies are cars driven by other people, that you must pay to do the driving on you behalf. For this reason, taxies are preferred by people who can't drive, don't want to drive, or shouldn't be allowed to drive, like children, bankers, drunks, and/or any combination of the three.

Taxi cabs also commonly include additional verbal services from the driver, ranging from small talk, to personal information, to *too personal* information, to opinions about 'immigration' that were recently acquired from the kind of newspapers that look like newspapers, but aren't.

BUSES

Buses are longer, cheaper, more sociable, less flexible taxis. Buses are considered to be very reliable at going where they are supposed to go, with many bus drivers boasting of the fact that they have so much experience driving their particular route, that it is almost impossible that they will get lost. This can be depressing to hear for train drivers, of course, who find it literally impossible to get lost, even when they try their very hardest.

Buses are, however, considered less reliable at getting where they need to go at the time they were supposed to go there, not because they stop to let people on and off, but because they must intermittently deal with the particularly faffy economic transactions of bus users.

This is why they are less favoured by important businessmen, because the important businessman's ability to be on time is undermined every time a tourist tries to pay the bus driver with a handful of pennies, old wooden buttons, or their library card.

TRAINS

Trains have three velocities: *forwards*, *backwards*, and *on strike*. The first two involve train drivers being generally well paid to go very fast in either direction, and the third involves them trying to be more well paid by going absolutely nowhere.

Train journeys are generally smooth, relaxing and comfortable, making them the perfect place to read a book, fall asleep, or simply stare out the window as a peaceful countryside floats lazily by, interrupted only occasionally by a loud, massive train suddenly and terrifyingly flying past in the opposite direction, five inches from your face.

Apart from when they are frequently not, trains are the most reliable method of getting somewhere fast. This is because, unlike buses and cars, their journey is very unlikely to be affected by the poor navigation skills of the driver, or the quality of driving exhibited by other train drivers.

Indeed, if they are being overtaken by other trains, there is quite obviously a serious problem which needs to be addressed, and train drivers will generally go on strike until they are more well paid to not understand it.

AIR PLANES

Air planes are like buses, except they don't stop to pick people up en route, because it's difficult to pick up new passengers without losing all of the old ones.

Travelling by air-plane has become increasingly popular throughout Human history, particularly when flights became cheap enough that you could afford return flights instead of just one-way ones. Before return flights became affordable, indeed, holidays were unpopular because every time you went on one you had to abandon all of your possessions and relationships forever.

Most flights are now shorter than the time you have to wait at the airport before you take them, so air planes should only be used as a way to cross larger distances or hop between separate land masses. Taking a flight to the office or the pub, for example, is discouraged, partly because you would have to land before where you took off just to slow down in time to disembark, and partly because it's clearly nonsense.

Compatibility
Connectivity Options Available

Relationships

Every time a new Human is created, it means they were the absolute best sperm out of several billion co-sperm. Every person on earth is therefore one of the most awesome possibilities imaginable – the fact that there's seven billion of the world's greatest sperm, all being people, all living side by side, all at once, is a magical coincidence. It's a planet full of winners.

It is no wonder, then, that many Humans like each other, and choose to celebrate this fact in various forms of relationship:

FRIENDS

When your Human collects another Human who shares similar views, this is called a *friendship*. With friends, it is much easier to believe that your Human is smart, funny, charming, and interesting, because you've surrounded yourself with a small bubble of people most likely to echo those qualities back at you. A friendship, then, is essentially a long series of obligations to meet up and agree with each other.

Some Humans even like agreeing with each other so much that they will travel long distances to visit and agree with each other, even when it would be much simpler for both of them to go door-to-door where they now live, and simply find a similar replacement.

Friendships can come in varying degrees of intensity, ranging from polite acknowledgement in a supermarket to showering together. The most intense friendships are those that only last a day, yet cover this whole spectrum. In general, friendships are ranked as follows:

Rank	Specific Roles
BOYFRIEND / GIRLFRIEND	Compliments, cuddling, advanced cuddling
BEST FRIEND	Obligations to do favours, gossip, banter, ceremonial functions

OLD FRIEND	Bearing witness to how much you've changed/grown; ignoring how much you've changed/grown; bringing up embarrassing past
NEW FRIEND	Chosen specifically because of shared interests/goals/post code; proof of ongoing likeability and/or proof of how hard it to say, "no, thanks, I have enough friends without you."
ONLINE FRIEND	Permanence; validation of your existence through 'commenting'

NEIGHBOURS

Although most models of Human don't realise it, their neighbours are incredibly important people in their lives, because the only thing preventing their complete entanglement with them is one brick-width's worth of wall. The ones who don't realise it, and never will realise it, have good neighbours. The ones who do realise it probably have the kind of awful neighbours that regularly come through their walls with a power drill.

ACQUAINTANCES

Acquaintances are people who live in the no-man's land between strangers and friends. These relationships are often charactered by small talk, awkwardness, and both party's unspoken acknowledgement that they quite like each other, but probably wouldn't have been aware if the other one had died any time in the last three decades.

STRANGERS

Humans that you don't know are very important, as they give the world that chaotic, detail-rich, 'hustle and bustle' feeling, which makes it seem so exciting and full of possibilities. Strangers allow you to go to concerts, and get lost in a crowd. Strangers allow you to go on holiday, and act like a moron. Strangers allow you to run marathons, and not lose. They're an essential lubricant to the world. For this reason, it is essential not to befriend everyone you meet or get too entangled with the lives of these replaceable shuffling anonymoids, but instead keep your distance, and allow strangers to retain their crucial strangeness.

ENEMIES

Enemies are neither friends nor strangers, but have many of the benefits of both. Not only can you dislike an enemy with the blind fervour you reserve for people you can't imagine, but you can also dislike them with the fully-sighted fervour of people you know quite well.

Enemies are a great way to keep busy and stay focussed, by allowing you to channel your Human's creative energy in ways that are intentionally counter-productive to someone else.

FAMILY

Family are strangers that normally become friends the minute you are born. The major disadvantage of families, of course, is that you don't get to choose them, making it a bit of a high-stakes lottery if you get a good one. However, it's best to remember that this element of the relationship works both ways. While a couple might choose to have a baby, they didn't get to choose that the baby would grow up to be you.

Helpful Tips

1	Smiling is an incredibly efficient way to optimise your life, because it makes people immediately see that you are happy, and want to be near you on the off-chance that your happiness is that rare contagious kind.
2	If someone insults you, the best way to redress the imbalance is not to insult them back, but, instead, to compliment them on how clever their insult was. This will induce pride, which will in turn induce sympathy, which will in turn make them want to invite you to their house. Once you're friends, steal their shoes.
3	A particularly effective method for nurturing contentment and even happiness in life is to *like yourself*. This is most easily achieved by trying to be a better person, and trying to do more good things. Good people are good, better people are better, and if you aren't either yet, at least you can't blame yourself for trying, you little underdog you.

Mating & Dating

SINGLEDOM

Singledom is considered one of the most free times of your Human's life, because you can do what they want, when you want, and you never have to report for cuddle duty, remember an anniversary, or share a bed. Loneliness can be particularly comfortable in big beds, and single people might prefer to enjoy more flamboyant sleeping positions while they still can. Popular choices include 'the sideways, diving scissors position', and 'the confused, fidgeting star-shape'. As for 'the funky swastika,' this has become an increasingly old-fashioned, out-dated and embarrassing position, mostly due to the rise of disco.

A lot of *being single* involves *trying not to be*, by going to the places where single people live. These are called *bars*. For this reason, most single people also prefer to have single friends, so they can all go out together, and help each other advertise their absolute singularity to strangers.

Old friends, in particular, make particularly good 'wingmen,' because they can offer up appealing anecdotes of past heroism like, "My friend is the most amazing person ever! I remember on my 15th birthday, they saved my building from a burning cat. What a hero!"

However, this level of intimacy can backfire when two single friends like the same potential stranger. This is when old friends make particularly bad 'wingmen,' because they also remember less appealing anecdotes like, "My friend is the most idiotic person ever! I remember on my 15th birthday, they tried to attach 15 lit candles to my cat. What a fire hazard!"

Being able to find out if another person is single is important, and can be accomplished in one of two ways. Either you can ask that person's friends directly, "is your friend single?", or, you can ask the person themselves indirectly. This is best achieved with more subtle questions like, "That looks like a nice drink you're drinking. Tell me, is that the kind of drink one might drink when one might also go home with me, please?"

DATING

While there are many different kinds of mating rituals practised in the animal kingdom, from inflating the body to look more impressive, to providing small gifts, to singing, to dancing, to waggling an impressively-coloured bum in the direction of a hopeful partner, Humans rarely do anything as sensible, unless they're in a nightclub.

Instead, you should try to find your Human a compatible partner through a long-winded and silly process called *dating*. Essentially, dating is when two people try to get to know each other, mostly by pretending to be two entirely better people for the duration of an evening.

To date effectively, two models of Human should sit on chairs opposite each other and broadcast the absolute best version of themselves that they can imagine. Simultaneously, they should become desperately receptive to the absolute best version that the other person is fabricating. Meanwhile, both should swallow unusual amounts of wine to confuse themselves. The best dates, consequently, are those where both Humans come out of it with a dopey grin, a feeling of hope, and a fatally distorted perception of what just happened.

This is why successful dating is often done as a *process*, with each subsequent date moving both partners slightly closer to reality.

RELATIONSHIPS

When two models of Human like each other enough, they become a one two-people person called a *couple*.

Being in a couple often means changing your life in lots of little ways to include your partner in it, and vise-versa. This is why every potential partner is not just a person to rub and share pancakes with, but an odd, lumpy, often unwieldy package of work obligations, family occasions, friend gatherings, and enemy sharing.

Indeed, being in a couple is about becoming so close that, even though you have two bodies, you feel like you have one brain. Good couples are like two people trying to remember anything that the other one might forget. Bad couples are like two people struggling to remember one piece of important information and blaming each other for not remembering the important piece of information. Oh, and the important information is where they left their baby.

Because of the amount of time Humans in relationships spend together, it is not uncommon for them to become so close they end up saying things like, "my partner is not just my lover, but also my best friend." This is sickly, but encouraged. However, people are warned against becoming so close that they say things like, "my partner is not just my lover, but also my best friend, postman, government, magician's assistant, and pet."

MARRIAGE

When two models of Human have been together long enough without any one better coming along, it is common for them to just give up and get married.

To celebrate this compromise, most Humans invite all of their friends and family members to a *wedding*, which is an expensive party designed to inform everyone of the decision, get some official men in fancy dresses in on the action, and show-off about your ability to make every single part of a whole day – invites, photos, bridesmaids, etc. - look somehow like a little girl's dream cake.

For almost everyone, the wedding is the best part of a marriage, because it is a whole day of socialising, dancing, eating, drinking, fun, friendship, and laughter which can be enjoyed by most of the people involved. This is, of course, excluding the catering, the bar staff, and the couple.

However, the day of the wedding also plays an important, ongoing role in every marriage as it provides a yearly opportunity to forget it. Humans forgetting their anniversaries is a common problem in relationships, normally with the one who wanted to have the nice day being angry with the other one who forgot. Weirdly, then, even though anniversaries also mean that two models of Human just did one more wondrous lap of the sun in each other's company, a popular way to celebrate is with a memorable argument about forgetfulness.

Helpful Tips

1	'Flirting' with other single people is fun, and best practised drunk.
2	The longer you are in a relationship, the more you will learn about how to please your partner in bed, such as by not hogging the duvet or spilling muesli on the pillows.
3	More impatient models of Human prefer to have an entire relationship in the condensed form of a *one-night stand*. This involves meeting each other, getting drunk, having sex, sharing a bed, sharing morning breath, sharing breakfast, getting sober, then realising the person is not the same person as when you first met and breaking up with them.

WARNING: PETS

Pets are nice animals that your Human might choose to name, invite home, and generally not eat. You should choose whether or not to have pets very carefully, because they are a big responsibility to feed, clean, and look after, but will not reciprocate these kinds of massive favour in any meaningful way.

Humans should also choose which species of pet to have carefully. If you want something just to look at, for example, a fish is ideal. However, if you want to run around, play with, and wrestle with the animal, you'll have a lot more success with your fish if you strap it first to a mammal of some kind.

Pets can be a wonderful addition to a life, offering almost limitless opportunities for exercise, responsibility, cuddles, hair, and getting out of social obligations. Indeed, when a pet-owning Human doesn't want to leave the comfort of their own home, they can simply use their animal as a great excuse, by saying something like, "oh, what a shame! I mean, I would absolutely loooooove to come to your afternoon choir performance on my only day off from work, but unfortunately my hamster is a hamster, so I can't."

The two most popular pets are *cats* and *dogs*, and there is a long-running argument about which one of them has the superior relationship with Humans. In general, dogs believe that cat owners are pointless and arrogant, whereas cats believe that dog owners are stupid and just want attention.

Of course, having a pet is also great practice for having a Human baby, except for the many, many ways that it isn't.

Storage
Best Stored In A Warm, Dry Place

Earth

When you leave a planet out in the sun for too long, it can go mouldy. This is called *life*, and is generally nothing to worry about. Indeed, sometimes life even turns into squirrels and Humans, which are fun.

The Earth is one such planet, and it is well-suited for hosting both squirrel and Human life. It's got wet stuff, hard stuff, magnets, lots of colours, a bit of history, nice views, a nearby moon you can visit, and not too many insects that are bigger than a shoe.

Indeed, Earth fits people so snugly that some models of Human have even theorised it was made just for them. Unfortunately, they arrived about 4.5 billion years too late to check if they were right.

Either way, this kind of belief is one that often passes with time. Some models of dinosaur, for example, also used to believe that the earth was created just for them, and now its very hard to find any that still do.

TEMPERATURE

You Human works best when stored in a cool, dry place, although should remain functional anywhere in your 'safe' temperature range, between *frozen* and *on fire*. Luckily, the earth is located at a very convenient distance from its main heating system, the Sun.

It is warm enough for your Human, meaning that water can exist all around you in its liquid form. It is also cool enough for your Human, meaning that you can hang out there and not feel embarrassed that other planets are judging you.

NUTRIENTS

Your Human's body has certain biological requirements because you are alive, a bit like a crab. Luckily, you can get all of these resources from *nature*, which still exists in several places and is often reachable by car.

In particular, the Earth's surface is covered in an abundance of fruit and vegetables, as well as all of the plants and animals needed for the production of sponge cakes, cappuccinos, and pina coladas.

GRAVITY

Earth has an absolutely lovely amount of its very own gravity, which works out great for people. They can run, jump, fall down, get up, and skip merrily, yet almost never fly off into outer space by accident. Gravity keeps your Human – and most of the stuff around you – conveniently attached to the ground, yet still allows you enough flexibility to throw things to, from and at each other when you are in a rush.

MOON

The Earth is also somewhat affected by the gravity of a moon, its moon, the Moon. This is particularly noticeable when you fall asleep on the beach but wake up in the sea. This water wobble is called a *tide*, and it is a great way to keep beaches clean and tidy, by twice a day removing all but the most unobservant and stubborn of visitors.

The moon can also be visited, of course, but wannabe tourists should remember that it's regarded as quite an expensive endeavour, and is therefore best undertaken only with a really, really good political motive, like winning.

SUNLIGHT

The sun is needed to keep plants and people awake during the day. Despite it being a terrifying and supermassive ball of nuclear fire, your Human is not always encouraged to completely hide from it.

Indeed, in moderation the sun can even be useful to your Human. While too much can certainly turn you radioactive and crispy, a little bit gives you Vitamin D, which prevents rickets; light, which prevents clumsiness; and tan-lines, which prevent a good tan.

Different places on Earth get varying amounts of sun, making it a planet very well suited for holidays. Humans in habitats with little sunlight are more likely to go on these holidays, whereas Humans in habitats with lots of sunlight are more likely to stay where they are instead, and have a whimsical attitude towards bedtime and GDP.

AIR

Without air to breathe in, your Human would have no air to breathe out, which would be disastrous for plants, trombonists, and people trying to cool down their soup. Luckily, air is in great supply all around the Earth, concentrated in convenient, accessible places called *skies*.

Your Human can breathe the sky in many different ways, depending on the type of air you want to get out of it. Really exciting air, for example, can be breathed in gasps, whereas bored and frustrated air should be let out in sighs.

Air is blue, flavourless, and highly addictive. Despite it being the chemical by-product of things like stinging nettles, seaweed and Christmas trees, it is completely safe for your Human to ingest, although some argue it causes a powerful hallucinogenic reaction called "reality" (don't worry, this hallucination ends when the effects of breathing wear off.)

You should breathe air whenever you feel like it, although you should give it maybe half an hour or so if birds have recently been swimming in it.

WATER

Your Human needs more water than anything else to survive. This is why people can so often be seen drinking, putting their heads into rivers, and complaining in the morning that sand is not a beverage. Luckily, water is available in a wide range of forms, including seas, rivers, melons, rain, taps, puddles, sweat, and foot-baths.

Due to concerns about safety and purity, some people do not like to drink tap water directly. These people often buy *bottled water* instead, which is water that comes from a tap indirectly, via a bottle.

Bottled water is believed by many models of Human to be of superior quality to tap water, however, as it comes pre-filtered. More specifically, it comes pre-filtered through an imaginary mountain spring and a corporate marketing department, before being bottled 'at source' (the tap) in natural and healthy plastic.

WARNING: THE ENVIRONMENT

Humans are very temporary creatures on a planet that is going to long out-live them, which has historically got them a bit muddled between the entirely related concepts of *wanting everything* and *consequences*.

Unfortunately, the mass production of everything Humans want has two by-products: *waste* and *pollution*. After spending quite a lot of time trying to hide these pesky consequences directly under the countryside in landfills so they didn't have to look at them, Humans are now increasingly encouraged to act in a way that treats their home a bit more like a home - a place where they live - and a bit less like the house party of someone they secretly hate - a place where they feel ethically fine drinking everything, breaking everything, weeing in the sink, and then leaving for a club once the ice runs out.

The biggest of these problems is *global warming*, where Humans (and cows) are causing the temperature of the earth to rapidly heat up. This causes ice to melt, and the sea level to rise, as things that used to live on that ice – like penguins and polars bears — fall into the water. This is a problem.

Luckily, most models of Human now agree that it is a problem, and are working on solving it at various speeds, ranging from almost casual indifference to urgent spectacular panicking.

The models of Human most likely to care about their home world becoming un-liveable are the ones who appreciate the attached context that there are not yet any alternative planets for them to live on, and that "the end of the world" also inevitably means the end of football, YouTube, and sausage rolls.

The Home: At a Glance

Ovens are the central point of the kitchen. They are primarily for heating food up, making it delicious, or simply for letting it cool down naturally, assuming the oven isn't turned on. Most Humans don't enjoy cleaning their ovens, so most Humans don't clean their ovens, which is fine.

Stairs are a way to get from one floor to another floor by building a whole bunch of small mini-floors in between them. These mini-floors are generally designed to be not much bigger than a couple of feet, otherwise they would all require furnishing and decorating.

Walls keep weather, strangers, and birds out of the house, whilst keeping warmth, possessions, and secrets in. While they are the main thing involved in transforming *nothing* into *a house*, they also play an important part in determining room size. Walls which are very close together create rooms ideal for toilets and storing golf clubs, whereas walls which are really far apart create rooms preferable for concerts, building Zeppelins, or living a boring, spacious existence in.

Fridges are the opposite of ovens, and can therefore be used to fix all of their mistakes. If your Human cooks something poorly, simply put it back into the fridge until the problem is undone, then try to cook it again. This can happen over and over again, which is how many generations of Human have learned to cook better recipes. In the rare case that there isn't any improvement in taste, food should instead be placed in the freezer, and cryogenically preserved for future generations to figure out.

Radiators are a clever system of pipes and metal containers for the easy transportation and storing of hot water, so you can always choose which one of the four seasons you would like your Human to live in. Most people choose to keep their homes at a constant year-long temperature of 'summer' because it is an effective way to dry laundry and it reminds them of holidays (especially holidays where you do a lot of laundry.)

Televisions are now a central feature of most homes. Despite this being a relatively recent development, television shows are now so evolved that they can entertain ordinary people by showing them unending footage of even more ordinary people, who are simply further away and therefore more exotic.

Pets are very popular kinds of furniture for some models of Human, because they move around the house and nobody is ever quite sure which part of it they're going to be in after a fireworks show.

Washing machines used to be seen as quite a revolutionary technology by the people who grew up without them. This is because of how much 'spare time' they suddenly created for the kind of normal people that would have previously spent 50% of their lives elbow-deep in a shed-load of sloppy vests. Now, however, the washing machine's incredible speed and power is rarely remembered or respected, except perhaps by the unlucky modern individuals who get stuck in them while they are on, and learn about washing machine *revolutions* the hard way.

Sinks are for washing hands, babies, plates, potatoes, and the hands of babies holding plates of potatoes. Most modern sinks have one tap which can release water ranging from cold to hot. Older sinks, however, have two taps, which allows the water to assume the quantum state of being *too hot, too cold* and *none of it just right,* simultaneously.

The Bed is the most beloved, cherished object in the life of any Human, although, ironically, they are rarely awake to enjoy them properly. Indeed, when they have the most time to enjoy them, they tend to fall asleep and waste the opportunity. And then, when they should stop enjoying them to go to work, this is the time you're most likely to see them clutching their duvet frantically like it's a life-boat in a storm.

Windows are transparent gaps in the walls of housing, which allow you to see where your house is every time your Human wakes up in it. If people don't like what is outside their windows, they can also place pictures and paintings over their windows. These will still look quite a bit like windows from the inside, but should instead foster the pleasant illusion that your house is surrounded not by its surroundings, but by a landscape of blurry French villages, or portraits of royalty, or endless bowls of dramatic fruit.

Doors are portals which facilitate you going from one room into another, therefore allowing you to forget why you did. Doors are what allow rooms in houses to have completely different purposes, so people don't have to sleep, cook, bathe and go to the toilet all in the same inter-connected space, but can nevertheless still visit other people who are sleeping, cooking, bathing and going to the toilet simply by pushing a bit of wood.

Tables are very popular pieces of furniture for a whole range of activities, including the steadying of food, leaning on, hiding stools, and storing items that have recently come out of pockets.

Gardens are small areas of enclosed land that you can use to water your Human's clothes and dry your Human's plants, or the other way around if you're not insane. Some traditional tribes of Human don't have a 'garden,' believing that a 'garden' is just a "man-made concept, man" and that "all of the earth, like, my garden, man". This is normally until they try to use all of the earth as their garden, and quickly find out that they've been surrounded by other Humans' fences and renamed a 'nature reserve.'

Lights transform your Human's home into a 24/7 non-stop indoor living-possibility theme park. Previously, when the sun went down, earlier models of Human simply had to put their life on pause and go to bed, or else wander bravely around the house holding a small candle, looking dramatic and old-fashioned. Now, lights create a whole night-time's worth of possibilities, including being visible enough for conversations, or inviting in theatrical moths for a nighty performance of the tragicomic masterpiece *The Moth and the Light Bulb*.

WARNING: TELEVISION

Humans are the only animals that care about what's going on in places they're not actually in. This is why every Human is required by law to have a television, so that they can try to watch everything that other Humans have pointed cameras at, all over the world, all day long, for all of their lives, pausing only occasionally for things like work, doorbells, sleep, adverts, and meals. Almost every Human must do this to at least some extent, or else they will have no idea what's going on in everyday conversation.

This has made some models of Human increasingly dependant on watching television to "stay informed," but increasingly clumsy at 'being a community.' This is because it is hard to find time to help your elderly neighbours do their shopping while you're trying to juggle your intellectual commitments to the thirty-nine separate political scandals, earthquakes, banking crises and revolutions that are happening in places you just found out existed this morning.

To "stay informed," you must constantly absorb something called *the news*. The news is essentially an unending, almost realistic soap opera of utter confusion, where an infinite amount of new story-lines and odd characters constantly emerge, develop, and intermingle. Despite this, watching the news causes many Humans to become incredibly opinionated, despite the fact their subconscious self is privately thinking something more like, "Wow. I have no idea what's going on. Who are all these people? Where is that place? When did *that* happen? Why don't I understand any of this? Does everyone else understand all this but me? I feel sad and silly and afraid."

Luckily, the news is also designed to be entertaining, which is why so few episodes of it are about the equally true but more mundane reality that almost all Humans, in almost all places, had a quite nice and completely ordinary day.

Living Arrangements

Due to the invention of locks, you can now choose relatively freely who you want to live with.

However, this privilege must nevertheless be earned, and your Human's living configuration is likely to change considerably over time, mostly in correspondence with your age, wealth, and relative uselessness:

LIVING WITH PARENTS

The first stage of most Humans' lives is spent living in the house of the people that decided that they should exist. At this point, Humans are completely dependant on their parents, which gives them the free time they need to play with toys, wobble around, and be generally too small.

In this unavoidable arrangement, none of the house belongs to the child - except perhaps for one small room - giving them little control over the decoration of the building. This is why most Human dwellings are mostly a boring combination of inter-linked squares and rectangles, painted beige with off-beige highlights, featuring samey, boring doors, instead of a much more interesting, sane and healthy mix of robot pirate ships, ballerina fairy castles, and dinosaur cowboy rainforest spaceships.

Living with your parents tends to become harder and harder as your Human gets increasingly closer to a similar height to them, and therefore starts questioning whether the authority should be redistributed somewhat more representatively in the relationship.

This is often an incorrect conclusion, mistaking the concept of *height* for the concept of *wisdom*. When teenagers crave the same kind of responsibility and respect as their elders, they often don't realise the full nature of this mistake until they're hit with their first post-load of work, banking, tax, and insurance documents. At this point, they normally try to renounce adulthood, revert back to their ignorant, irresponsible bliss, and hide under their childhood blankets until they can be lured out again around age 16 with the offer of a car.

LIVING WITH PEERS

Upon *moving out*, some models of Human choose to live with their friends and peers, either to be sociable, save money, or have emotional support when encountering new adult problems like what to do with a bin when it is suddenly full. This type of living situation is therefore popular with *young adults* only, mainly for the reason that old adults used to be young adults, and therefore realise how much they would now hate living with the kind of person they used to be.

It is particularly common for students to live together, as they thrive most in an environment where different academic disciplines can share ideas and theories in the pursuit of mutual intellectual progress. Indeed, if you put a Social Sciences student, an Anthropology student, a Philosophy student, and a Literature student all together in the same student house, it normally only takes a few months of intense debate before they figure out how to turn the washing machine on.

LIVING ALONE

When you first live alone, you Human normally experiences an unprecedented level of personal freedom. This is because you no longer have to follow other people's rules, but can instead start following rules set by yourself. For most Humans, rules set by themselves are often far more agreeable than external ones, as they tend to have a fluffier nature, such as, *Rule 27: You may wear only pants*, and, *Rule 19: Yes cake is breakfast.*

Living alone also has many of the other consequence-free advantages associated with nobody being around to judge you, including accidental naps, intentional untidiness, snoring, burping, farting, regular confused muttering, and justification-free nudity during the preparation of milkshakes.

Living alone is also a great option for models of Human who are not quite ready to share their movie collection with another person, until that person has proven that they definitely, definitely understand the finer nuances between the "Action Thriller" and "Thriller, with Action" sections of the classification system.

LIVING WITH A PARTNER

Choosing to move in with a partner is a big step, and an important test for any relationship, because it is the first time that relationship has had to survive the sharing of a sink.

Many relationships break up, many buy dishwashers, and many more buy dishwashers then continue to have similar arguments about who was the last one to empty it. These kinds of couples often have to go to special *dishwasher couples therapy*, where they are continuously shown traumatic photos of the dirty, dish-filled sinks of their past, until they can finally reconcile over the shared memory of how horrible washing up used to be.

To begin living together, one Human can either move in with the other one, or both can move into a new empty place simultaneously. This latter option is often preferable as it gives both partners equal information about where everything they own is going to be stored. This prevents the most common argument of all, which occurs when one partner tidies away Thing from the place Thing normally is, and has always been, to a new place, where Thing normally isn't, then forgets the new location of Thing, thus effectively banishing Thing forever to The Forgotten Realm of Eternal Location-less Purgatory (normally a drawer.)

LIVING WITH CHILDREN

Humans have children when they finally decide they have become uncool enough to be like their parents.

Coincidentally, this is also the point that many Humans realise they were wrong about who held the power in the parent-child relationship. While they may have previously believed that their parents told them what to do all day long, now that they are parents they suddenly realise that children decide when adults wake up, what time adults can go to sleep, and roughly what mood adults are going to be in for most of the day.

Habitats

Humans try to live everywhere, from mountains to deserts to ice tundras, depending mostly on what they want to see when they look out of the window. Indeed, there are even models of Human that live under the sea in submarines and Humans that live over the sky in space stations, so they can look out of the window and mostly decide to not go for a walk.

This adventurous, pioneering spirit is partly because Humans like a challenge. If you do like a challenge, of course, you won't find much that is more challenging than discovering a challenging environment, then deciding to live in it. However, an odd thing happens when a child is born in a challenging environment: they no longer see it as *challenging*, just as *normal*. This explains why so many models of Human still insist on living in absolutely rubbish places like mountains and deserts and ice tundras and horrifying suburbs, even after you show them photographs of beach bars in Costa Rica.

Indeed, it is almost universally common for Humans to stay roughly in the area they were born, as this is where they feel the most sensible and comfortable. They speak the local language, understand the local culture, and have the most relevant geographical knowledge of the local area. Choosing to leave the safety of your language and local understanding, therefore, is essentially choosing to revert back to the status of a child, and look like an idiot to everyone around you, which you may still often want to do. This is called *tourism*.

One of the most important factors affecting where Humans generally live relates to resources. The most popular Human settlements were all established because of their proximity to rivers, arable land, or the likelihood of future airports.

Settlements

Humans have a natural tendency to gather into groups.

The reason for this is simple: if two people stop to chat by a river, for example, then whoever walks past next is likely to be curious enough about what is going on to stick around, and see what happens next. Three people standing around near a river is even more intriguing, of course, so the fourth and fifth passing Human are also likely to stop and watch, just in case something good happens. Eventually, this boring process of mostly nosiness leads to civilisation.

Humans tend to live together in communities of varying sizes, depending on how many of their neighbours they don't want to know.

VILLAGES

Villages can have very few people, or quite a lot of people, as long as they are surrounded by lovely cows. The only villages that should be avoided at all costs are the ones that have quite a lot of people, very few surnames, and cows that look at those people in a vaguely haunted way.

Despite their relative isolation, villages are highly-advanced hubs of communication. If there is gossip about someone in the village, this information is distributed instantly and efficiently to every other person in the village through dog-walk small-talk and beer-soaked pub-drunk blabbering. This is why there is less internet access in the countryside – it's too slow. It's also too boring, as real news doesn't have the same quality as village 'news', which is a thousand billion exaggerations more exciting, especially once it's been passed through the brains of people that not a huge amount happens to.

Indeed, if you stumble over a dog on one side of the village, it's likely the other side will hear a rumour that you died in a sky-diving accident before you've even touched the ground.

TOWNS

Towns were originally built on roads so there was somewhere to stop when you were on the way from somewhere to somewhere, and wanted to buy stuff in between. As such, the central point of most towns is the high street, which is a collection of shops built alongside the main road, so that essential items like milk, bread, haircuts and gambling can be purchased from a moving car, simply by leaning out of the window and wildly grabbing in the direction of the shop-keeps.

Towns are not small enough for their residents to know everyone in them, but are small enough that you're likely to see the same kinds of people in the same kinds of places, whether you want to or not. While this generally means you're likely to have old and reliable town-based friendships, it also means you're likely to live amongst friends that know how old and unreliable you are. This makes it relatively difficult to suddenly reinvent yourself. It's hard to fulfil your wish to become an international teen-pop sensation if everyone around you knows that you're a 54 year-old carpenter called Big John.

People from small towns can also be afflicted by something known as 'small town syndrome,' which often manifests itself as a fear of outsiders, change, city dwellers, unexplained hair styles, and music that is a bit faster than the music their parents were afraid of. The cure for 'small town syndrome' is to travel to other parts of the world, creating the refreshing opportunity to let other people from small towns be afraid of you.

CITIES

Cities are like a whole collection of towns, all in one place, sprinkled with pollution, and wrapped lovingly in an unreliable motorway. The majority of Humans live in cities, which means they're a great place to go if you're a big fan of strangers. Cities were invented because they were a convenient place to source workers, collect taxes, distribute post, and make friends. Meanwhile, there were so many names written on maps, that it seemed a shame not to put places on them, especially as those places would be so easy to find.

Cities tend to be the busiest places on earth, due to their high-density populations being contained in relatively small geographic areas. Indeed, there are sometimes so many Humans in such a small area that the only vaguely appealing way to fit them all in is to keep stacking them on top of each other in vertical storage containers called *sky-scrapers*. Sky-scrapers are also the best places in every city to enjoy unrestricted, breath-taking views, unless, of course, you don't live in the skyscraper, in which case your views are often restricted by breath-taking skyscrapers.

Cities also offer your Human a wide range of character-building services and opportunities, including jobs, crime, concerts, dating, noise, parks (which are like the countryside, except with a fence, roller-skaters, and a closing time), and frequent exposure to tourists.

City residents often have a difficult relationship with tourists, because tourists tend to visit their city and do incredibly annoying, out-of-place things like "enjoy themselves" and "appreciate it," which is missing the point. Of course, if you really wanted to have the kind of "authentic experience of the city" that tourists often crave, the best way is to move there, live there, then think constantly about leaving.

WARNING: FUTURE MODELS

It is not exactly certain what future models of Human will think, look like and be able to do, because of how exponentially quickly they keep coming up with crazy new ideas, materials, and confusing new technology.

However, this is nothing new, and also nothing to worry about. Indeed, it has always been the case that Humans were terrible at predicting the future. If you asked a Human two hundred years ago what you could invent for them to help with their day-to-day life, they wouldn't have said, "plastic," "laptops," "pre-sliced cheese," "laser eye surgery," "the fridge," and, "satellites." No. In fact, they would have been particularly forward-thinking if they had said "brighter candles" or "a less grumpy horse."

The same is true today. Humans may know that they've got a few potential challenges on the horizon to solve, but they don't yet know what kinds of tools and ideas they're going to have on-hand to solve these challenges with. It is therefore important for you to remember that the future of the species has not yet been decided as 'doomed', regardless of how much you google things, but remains a specactularly unfathomable soup of bizarre and beautiful possibilities, still open for all ideas, suggestions, friendly feedback, and helpful nudges in the right direction.

Cynics should, of course, feel equally free to enjoy their cynicism. They should merely be asked to enjoy it a little more quietly, so as not to distract the idealists from fixing things.

DISCLAIMER

While we hope that this manual will help you to get a fun, healthy and vaguely useful life out of your Human, we nevertheless apologise that there will be inevitable occasions when things go a bit weird or wonky due to the unpredictable nature of Human's inbuilt *Free Will*™ technology.

Unfortunately, due to the almost limitless power that you have over your own perception of reality, at this time we are not able to take any further responsibility for your Human once it is no longer in its original packaging (or "mother"). Once *Free Will*™ technology has been activated*, your Human can no longer be sent back, rebuilt, reformatted, or replaced. Its yours, and only yours, for good.

(*Please note: If you want to make the age-old complaint that your Human has never had *Free Will*™, we would respectfully remind you that this is, ahem, *your choice*, and that no refunds can or will be given in universes where all events are pre-determined. Any such complaint will simply be reported as 'your destiny', unfortunately.)

Luckily, the real joys, motivations and rewards of operating a Human don't come from waking up every day then randomly flinging your limbs and opinions in all directions. Instead, they come from carefully and cleverly exploring the almost infinite salad of possibilities offered by being able to choose the life that you want to live

Please remember, though, that every available Human is a completely unique, funny, interesting, peculiar and wonderful model that will never exist again. It is therefore important in order to get the most enjoyment out your life as humanly possible, that you make this choice yourself.

Good luck, have fun, and please enjoy your time on planet earth.

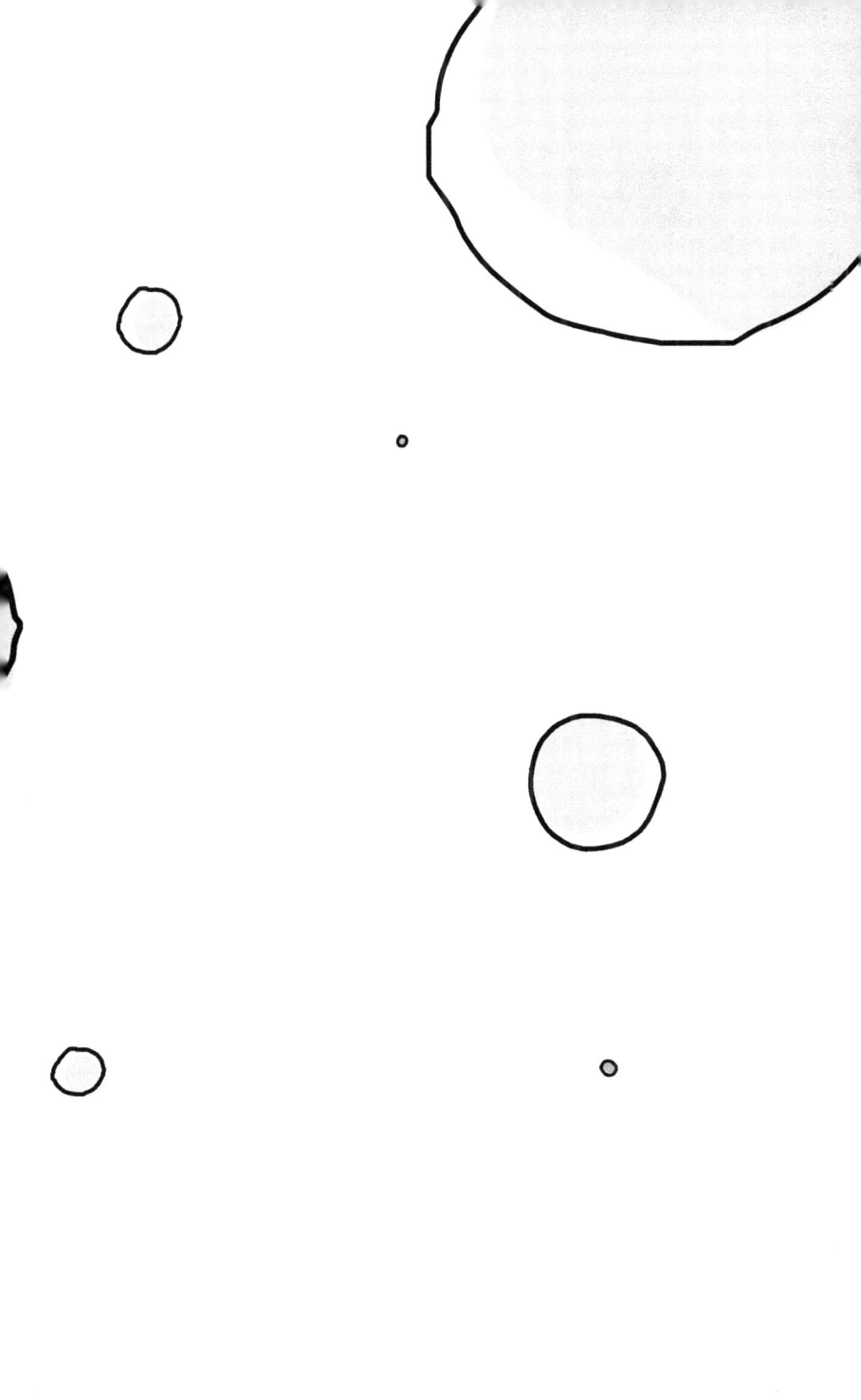

ABOUT THE AUTHOR

Paul Hawkins is a British comedy writer and illustrator, living in Germany. His background is mostly in film, scriptwriting, and trying to avoid responsibility whenever it rears its ugly head. His main ambition, indeed, is to retire. To this end, his life-long pilgrimage to avoid a 'proper' job has brought him to the Holy Mecca of Delayed Responsibility: Berlin. He is the co-author of the *Der Spiegel* best-selling book *Denglisch for Better Knowers* (2013), and author of *iHuman/Gebrauchsanleitung Mensch* (2014), *Dealing with Adulthood/ Erwachsenwerden für Anfänger* (2016), and the upcoming book, *How to Take Over the Earth* (2017). You can follow his "work" or find out more about him at:

www.paul-hawkins.com

You can also contact him directly at *paul@hencewise.com*, or via his literary agent - a nice man called Frank - at Landwehr & Cie.

graphic editing: Agnese Laguzzi / www.visual-concept-design.de

Logbook

www.ingramcontent.com/pod-product-compliance
Lightning Source LLC
Chambersburg PA
CBHW060158050426
42446CB00013B/2881